BATTLE
OF THE
SEXES
IN THE ANIMAL WORLD

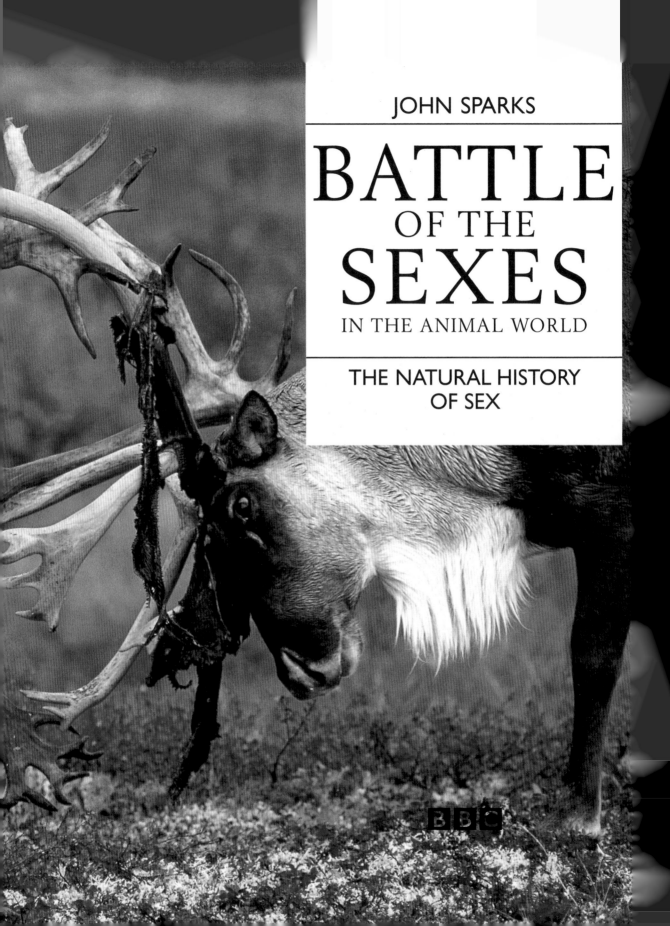

JOHN SPARKS

BATTLE
OF THE
SEXES
IN THE ANIMAL WORLD

THE NATURAL HISTORY
OF SEX

BBC

FRONTISPIECE Head to head combat. The weapons
of war for male caribou are huge antlers used to twist
and throw their opponent off balance.

PAGE 6 It pays to be bullish: male musk oxen
batter each other with their enormous, thick skulls.
The strongest head-banger wins the females.

This book is published to accompany the television series
Battle of the Sexes in the Animal World,
which was produced by the BBC Natural History Unit, Bristol,
and first broadcast on BBC 2 in 1999.
Series Producer: John Sparks
Producers: Hilary Jeffkins, John Ruthven, Phil Savoie and Julian Hector

Published by BBC Worldwide Ltd,
Woodlands, 80 Wood Lane, London W12 0TT

First published 1999
© John Sparks 1999
The moral right of the author has been asserted.

ISBN: 0 563 37145 5

Commissioning editor: Sheila Ableman
Project editor: Martha Caute
Text editor: Caroline Taggart
Art director: Linda Blakemore
Designer: Rachel Hardman Carter
Picture researcher: Frances Abraham

Set in Berling Roman
Printed and bound in France by Imprimerie Pollina S.a.
Colour separations by Radstock Reproductions Ltd, Midsomer Norton
Jacket printed in France by Imprimerie Pollina S.a.

CONTENTS

ACKNOWLEDGEMENTS

This book was written at the same time as a series of the same title was being produced for BBC Television. Although I have been fortunate enough in over thirty years of film-making and travelling for the BBC's Natural History Unit to have witnessed some of the activities covered in the following pages, in very many instances, I have had to base my accounts on detailed descriptions and interpretations published in learned zoological journals and elsewhere. These sources are too numerous to record in a book of this nature. As a consequence, like anyone else involved in writing for a general readership, I am hugely indebted to a vast number of dedicated naturalists and distinguished scientists who have painstakingly pieced together the complexities of how animals conduct their lives. They have made a valuable contribution to our knowledge of the way in which the natural world works, and I have drawn heavily upon their discoveries.

Battle of the Sexes has benefited enormously from being closely involved with the TV series because, during the course of arranging expeditions the world over to film the animals which played a key role in the story, many scientists generously shared their knowledge and expertise with us. Without them, our task would have been immeasurably more difficult. Among those to whom I should like to express my thanks are: in the UK – Dr Tim Clutton-Brock, Dr Nick Davies FRS, Dr James Deutsch, Professor Robin Dunbar, Professor Tim Halliday, Professor W.B. Hamilton FRS, Mary Hector, Dr Thibaud Monin, Dr Peter Parks, Dr Marion Petrie, Paddy Pomeroy, R. & K. Preston-Mafham, Dr Francis L.W. Ratnieks, Dr Rosanna L. Robinson, Dr Professor M. Siva-Jothy, Anthony Smith, Dr G.F. Turner; in Sweden – Dr Bengt Silverin; in Australia – Annette Cooper, Dr A.G. Orr, Dr Tony Friend, Professor Roger V. Short, Dr Leigh Simmons; in Papua New Guinea – Dr Frank Bonaccorso, Bruce Beehler; in the USA – Professor Dan Costa, Dr Marc S. Dantzker, Dr Erika Deinert, Professor Bill Eberhard, Dr Walter D. Koenig, Dr Roy W. McDiarmid, Professor David McDonald, Professor Barry Sinervo, Dr Bruce J. Turner, Professor Gerald Wilkinson; in Kenya – Dr Joyce Poole; in South Africa – Professor Jenny Jarvis, Dr Phillip Richardson, Dr Steven R. Telford; in Austria – Michael Taborsky, Drs Jorge and Martha Hendrichs and Dr Herbert Hoi.

No single person can take credit for a television project. *Battle of the Sexes* is no exception. As Series Producer, I should like to pay tribute to the production team, all the members of which were as enthusiastic as they were talented. Holly Spearing undertook some preliminary research for the series before the producers – Hilary Jeffkins, John Ruthven, Phil Savoie and Julian Hector – were enlisted. Their pursuit of new and fascinating film sequences both enhanced the six episodes, and influenced what I wrote. To them, and to other members of the team – Lucy Crowe, Bernadette John-Lewis, Angie Lance and Sally Cryer – I should like to express my sincere appreciation.

My first drafts left much room for improvement, and I am especially indebted to Julian Hector – a research zoologist before he took up broadcasting – who assiduously read them, corrected my errors and made numerous and extremely valuable suggestions for clarifying the text. Needless to say, any shortcomings which remain are mine.

It has been a pleasure to work with BBC Books, and in particular with Sheila Ableman, Martha Caute, Linda Blakemore, Rachel Hardman Carter and Caroline Taggart; and I should like to thank Frances Abrahams for discovering so many wonderful photographs to bring the text to life.

And lastly, an acknowledgement to my wife Sara, as ever a source of constant encouragement, who for long stretches of time saw only my back as I crouched over the keyboard and silver screen of the word processor.

John Sparks
Bristol

INTRODUCTION

Every living creature has an overwhelming urge to breed. This is not simply a trivial expression of bestial lust, but a fundamental characteristic of life, the fulfilment of which determines whether an animal is a success or a failure. 'Succeeding', in evolutionary terms, means nothing more nor less than leaving offspring who will survive long enough to carry on the parents' line. Anything less means the extinction of their own genetic heritage. Each individual therefore strives to populate the planet with its own descendants at the expense of those of its rivals. And in order to do so, each and every one of them attempts to attain reproductive supremacy by means of the sexual process.

The nature of sex is widely misunderstood, a matter which this book will attempt to rectify. The human ideal of sex is that it is the romantic outcome of love and leads the participants into a long-term alliance, enabling them to produce and rear children – an arrangement that is all too often shattered in the divorce courts. And yet a wealth of observation on how animals conduct their private lives shows that – in the wild – sexual skulduggery and infidelity are much more the norm than the exception. Sex does not and never did encourage sharing and caring. On the contrary, as the story which unfolds in the next six chapters reveals, it compels the participants to engage in civil war at all stages of their lives. Although mates consent to donate eggs and sperm towards the creation of new life, on almost every other issue – the choice and number of partners, the size of their families and who is going to look after them – males and females are far from agreement. Even when the sexes appear to co-operate, powerful forces of self-interest are at work. The relationship between the genders is constantly rife with tension and mistrust. Why should this be so?

Ideally, every individual, whether male or female, would like to mix and match its genes with the best of its kind to create the healthiest and sturdiest offspring – a recipe for their survival. This aspiration involves females in a quest to find the perfect sexual partner – perhaps the most elegant dancer, the most accomplished hunter or simply the biggest and most belligerent male. Once she has found him, she may resort to various forms of subterfuge in order to keep him – and his genes – to herself. Males, on the other hand, generally try to give themselves the best chance in the reproductive stakes by mating with as many females as possible.

In addition to this basic conflict of interest, the problem is that someone else always seems to have the best mate. Of course, there is no such thing as a faultless female or an impeccable male; however, when animals are set on breeding, they frequently appear to behave as though they have settled for second-best while continuing to keep their options open – in other words they divorce, swap partners and have affairs. Throughout the animal kingdom, males have inherently roving eyes, are ever ready to cheat on their partners and are accordingly paranoid about being cuckolded themselves. Females are also open to offers from males more desirable than the ones with whom they have paired up, and they use infidelity as a weapon in the battle of the sexes. All this sexual skulduggery leads to discord, as animals of every kind strive to ensure the survival of as many of their genes as possible.

The very concept of sex also calls for explanations. Intercourse is mechanically cumbersome and does not necessarily result in a net increase in numbers. Budding or cloning would seem, at first glance, to be much more effective ways of propagation. Without a doubt, sex in its various manifestations involves the expenditure of huge amounts of energy. For some animals, it shortens life expectancy; it is sometimes even lethal, usually for males but occasionally for females as well. So why do it? We shall look at some of the possible answers to these questions in Chapter 6.

Sex and foraging are two fundamental characteristics of animal life, and are often the only ones which draw creatures out into the open. Sex especially demands very public behaviour among many species. Males and females need to find each other, repel rivals, court, make the sexual connection and provide for their young. However, in taking such a high profile, they face the danger of being hunted or sexually cheated. Individual species have inevitably evolved their own strategies for dealing with these risks, and these strategies have fashioned the dazzling array of individual species which share our planet. For all of them, sex is a continuing battle.

I

WARRIORS
AND WIMPS

The recurring theme of this book is that the opportunities created by sex differ for males and females. The reason for this asymmetry lies in the nature of their respective sex cells – sperm and eggs. Sperm are minuscule, biologically 'cheap' to manufacture, and are produced by the testes in astronomical numbers. Eggs, on the other hand, are comparatively large – small humming-birds, for instance, make eggs equivalent to 25 per cent of their body weight and packed with nutrients. Being 'expensive' to make, they are produced in much smaller numbers than sperm. The consequences for the two sexes are profound. With a more or less fixed output of eggs, females cannot usually generate more offspring by taking on extra mating partners. Their best option is to be careful in their choice of who fathers their young. Males have quite a different agenda. With an almost unlimited supply of sperm at their disposal, their best reproductive strategy is to mate with as many females as possible, each of which will provide them with offspring.

PREVIOUS PAGES
Fighting flies. Male antler flies are equipped with weapons like miniature stags and joust for sexual dominance. The winner will be the one that mates with the unadorned females.

From a male's perspective, there are never enough females to go around and so, motivated by lust and sheer greed, each of them comes into serious competition with other philanderers. To be successful in the mating stakes, a male needs to win and win well. This rivalry manifests itself as raw aggression among the sturdy males of those species for which 'biggest is best'. To be triumphant in battle, a male has to look like a warrior, act like a warrior – and mean it!

Competition for sex is the overriding evolutionary pressure responsible for fashioning the appearance of mature males, whether they be chest-thumping gorillas or heavily veiled fighting fish. This is because, in the struggle for supremacy, weapons and large body size have been overwhelmingly advantageous, enabling hefty, well-armed males to win more mates than feeble and less bold ones. Over countless generations, macho males driven by their gonads have been willing to risk life and limb in order to rank among the most bountiful breeders of their kind. Such a valuable prize is always worth fighting for, and only the most pugilistic individuals stand a chance of winning – which is why the males of many species are larger and more irascible than their mates. To help them in their battle against rivals, warrior males throughout the animal kingdom have often become heavyweights, equipped with weapons enabling them to stab, ram, kick or wrestle. For those which compete for harems, the reward for being a successful male is proportionately high, and so the conflicts become that much more serious.

When a pair of bull elephant seals clash on the breeding beaches, no quarter is given. Each is a warrior fighting for the survival of his line. By far the largest of the seals, each bellowing bull is a quivering mound of flesh and blubber 6 metres (20 feet) long and weighing 3000 kilograms (6600 pounds) – five times the weight of a mature female. His huge head is made all the more grotesque by an inflatable proboscis that dangles over his open mouth. This is a kind of trumpet which resonates to the bull's battle cry, helping to strike terror into all who challenge him. But bull elephant seals in their prime are not faint-hearted. Facing each other in combat, they rear up and lunge at each other, each animal shuddering under the impact of the other's blows. As the fight proceeds, they become increasingly blooded. Their canine teeth, although small and blunt, can inflict gruesome-looking gashes on a rival's neck, which is heavily reinforced with blubber to take the worst out of the vicious lunges. Even so, the combatants often tear their noses and gouge out chunks of their opponent's skin. There is a lot at stake, and well-matched rivals do not give up easily. But inevitably, one of them backs off and awaits a further opportunity to challenge the beachmaster.

Male elephant seals have invested all their energy on bulk and aggression to win access to females. They make no contribution to rearing the pups – indeed the young, which are tended by the beachmaster's females, were conceived the previous year, almost certainly by a different bull. Whereas every cow which survives to maturity will reproduce, the odds are heavily stacked against the males. Fewer than one in ten become successful warriors commandeering their own stretches of the beach favoured by the females; the rest will die without issue or resort to sneaking a furtive mating here and there. Competition between the lusty males is therefore intense, and success will favour only the heaviest and most belligerent of them – thus accounting for the huge difference in size between the sexes in this species.

And yet the bulls can grow too big for their own good! In Northern Californian elephant seals, about one in a thousand cows dies during the act of copulation, each suffocated by the crushing weight of the bull on her back. Although this may not seem like a serious death rate, the risk to the cows is sufficiently high for some to seek sex with smaller bulls, usually while the giants are slugging it out among themselves! So the super-aggressive behaviour of the beachmasters gives some wimpish males a chance to spread their characteristics, and this checks the evolutionary trend towards ever larger and more brutish males.

In elephant seal society, the winning warriors are amply rewarded. The most dominant beachmasters in the South Georgia population have harems of between ten and twenty cows, all of which they will inseminate, thus passing on their characteristics to a clutch of pups. However, staving off challenges and a surfeit of sex takes its toll, and a bull can expect to breed for only a year or two before being beaten by younger and more virile males.

There is no universal technique for becoming a champion fighter. Fish bite and erect their fins. Carnivores and many monkeys such as baboons raise their hackles and use their teeth. Kangaroos and moorhens strike out with their legs, the former delivering powerful kicks to the opponent's belly and the latter grappling with the feet. Zebra stallions not only lash

Horns and antlers

out with their hind legs but also try to nip their opponents. Rival snakes, seals and giraffes engage in bouts of neck wrestling, whereas male chameleons gain the upper hand by forcing an opponent off the branch. Ring-tailed lemurs indulge in stink fights, anointing their 'feather-duster' tails with scent from their wrist glands and wafting it in each other's faces.

Among the invertebrates, some male beetles, such as stag and Hercules beetles, take on the appearance of medieval knights, bristling with murderous-looking projections from the front of their armoured bodies. The males of these insects engage in jousting matches using their weapons to grasp and lever their rivals, eventually heaving them aside. Some very unusual Diopsid flies have conspicuous paired projections coming out of their cheeks rather like antlers. They vary in shape from species to species, resembling the flattened antlers of moose, the branched ones of deer and the coiled horns of rams.

LEFT Clash of the titans: warrior male elephant seals battle for sexual supremacy. These clashes are the most awesome in the animal world and often result in severe injuries.

BELOW No holds barred: male stag beetles (below left) and poison dart frogs (below right) wrestle for dominance and the right to mate.

Apparently, males do not need these curious outgrowths in order to win fights, but those without them expend much more effort before their conflicts are resolved.

The most spectacular horns and antlers adorn the heads of the hoofed mammals. They come in an amazing array of shapes and sizes, resembling corkscrews, rapiers, daggers and meat hooks; some are tightly spiralled, others extravagantly branched. In many cases, the females are hornless, but when horns are present in both sexes, as in the larger antelopes, the females use them as stabbing weapons in the event of having to defend their calves. Those sported by the bulls are fighting weapons employed during the rut to further their owner's breeding ambitions. The male's adornments are constructed on a more massive scale than those of the female, and their complex shape is generally designed to parry and fend off the blows of an opponent during head-to-head encounters. In deer, where the stags have deciduous antlers, or in antelope, sheep and wild cattle, where the bulls possess permanent horns, the fights take the form of trials of strength with the combatants pushing against each other with all their might. Nevertheless, ibex, big-horn sheep, goats and musk oxen perform serious battering contests in which the opponents gallop towards each other and meet head on; it is a wonder that any participant survives such head-shattering impacts.

The secret of their survival lies in the construction of their skulls. Like the other head bangers, bull musk oxen possess skulls like crash helmets which act as shock absorbers for cushioning the delicate brain tissue. The forces generated are considerable: the bone dome of the big-horn sheep, for instance, can withstand a blow sixty times that required to fragment a human skull – an achievement made possible by the extremely crenellated sutures between the bones which allow the plates to move and dissipate much of the shock of the collisions.

Examples like these show how males of all kinds have become embroiled in an arms race favouring those which can grow and deploy ever bigger weapons. The extinct Irish elk was one such species: the older stags sported a mighty spread of antlers that would dwarf those of modern deer. Like those of today's warriors, such weapons are costly to grow – especially those of deer, which have to be regrown every year – and the individual has to be a very competent forager to find enough food to be able to 'afford' to replace them annually. The antlers must therefore double up as truthful indicators of the male's general vigour and fitness, as well as being effective in combat.

And yet fights do occasionally escalate, especially among harem-holding mammals such as wapiti and elephant seals, and fatal injuries are not unknown.

Stags sometimes sustain smashed antlers or broken legs, or are blinded in one eye. In one population, battles over rutting supremacy accounted for 20 per cent of all adult male mortality and in Germany 5 per cent of stags are killed every year through fighting. Some 10 per cent of bull musk oxen die from fractured skulls, despite the reinforced nature of their foreheads, and no less than 60 per cent of narwhals sport broken tusks or have pieces of twisted ivory buried in their flesh – doubtless all wounds incurred through fighting.

In some species, advertising powerfulness is a more effective way of competing than actual battle. 'Sabre-rattling' shows of strength by posturing, and wars of nerves in which the tension is kept taut, are ways of daring the opposition to fight without necessarily staking one's life. Such rituals enable males to launch themselves into combat only after carefully weighing up the odds of winning.

Posturing and choral warfare

A stag wapiti in the prime of life is one of the most impressive creatures to be seen in North America. With huge ruffed shoulders, and head crowned by magnificently branched antlers, he is built for battle. Yet he rarely needs to put his potentially lethal weapons to the test because wapitis have developed an effective way of weighing up their chances of succeeding in a challenge. They do so by bugling for all they are worth – the more frequent the calling and the longer the individual bugles, the larger and more confident the challenger. On hearing such a battle cry, many stags concede defeat, presumably because they judge the opposition to be stronger than themselves. If neither stag backs down, they size each other up by walking in parallel to show off their powerful profiles. Many male mammals, such as bison, lions and sacred baboons, 'puff' themselves up with hairy capes to exaggerate the size of their bodies and make themselves look more daunting. The elongated hair on the wapiti's neck and shoulders has the same effect. Only if neither stag withdraws do they resort to a mighty clash of antlers in which, even after such a careful assessment of each other, either contender may be wounded.

During the rut, red deer stags also engage in prolonged vocal contests. In fact, roaring is a good indicator of fighting ability because continuous calling takes a great deal of stamina, signalling that the stag must be in the peak of health. And yet there is a cost to all this strutting. During the rutting season, the top harem-holding males are bellowing at intruders day and night, and this prevents them from feeding. Ultimately they lose both their condition and their vocal edge, enabling fitter young stags to take over their hinds, but not until after they have managed to make most of them pregnant.

Deer are not the only animals to use their voice as a form of choral warfare. The volume of a lion's roar, the intensity of a bull sperm whale's clicks and the strength of a cock bird's song tells a great deal about the status and vigour of the vocalist. The pitch of a toad's croak also gives away his size – the deeper the croak the heavier his body and so it pays potential rivals to listen first before wrestling over a female.

Eye-ball to eye-ball

Rivalry over sex is responsible for the evolution of some of the strangest shaped bodies. Stalk-eyed flies are among the most extraordinary of all insects. Between 5 and 10 millimetres (¼–½ inch) long, they inhabit the lush vegetation around the edges of tropical streams and rivers where they swarm at dusk on rootlets that hang underneath banks. In these insects there is a skewed sex ratio with a surfeit of females, and the males compete among themselves for as many of them as possible. As a broad head is an indicator of body size and so of fighting strength, stalk-eyed flies have evolved a fascinating method of intimidating an opponent by placing the eyes out on stalks. Both sexes possess

Eyeing up the opposition: stalk-eyed fly males assess each other's vital statistics. The one with eyes furthest apart wins the contest – and the females.

eye stalks, but those of the males are incredibly long, about the length of the fly's body, so that the span of both stalks is equivalent to twice the body length. The larger the fly, the longer its stalks. With such widely spaced eyes, males have excellent binocular vision and are able to assess the size of a challenger when he is up to a metre (over 3 feet) away.

But inevitably, after eyeballing each other, males with similar eye spans approach head to head. While duelling, they are able to evaluate their relative sizes directly by lining up their heads to assess which has the wider-set pair of eyes. If they are more or less equal, they rise up on their mid and hind legs, spread their forelegs alongside their eye stalks and, in a series of very rapid lunging movements, attempt to displace each other. In nine out of ten cases, the heavier fly with the greater eye separation wins the day. The males with the longer eye stalks also have hardier sperm and will sire more offspring.

Stalk-eyed fly behaviour is an amazing example of risk assessment where even a relatively primitive creature with a simple nervous system turns out to be a master of weighing up the odds of success. The behaviour has been fashioned by evolution; after all, endlessly engaging in duels which neither individual can win is completely counter-productive. But balancing aggressive posturing with warrior-like attacks is smart for males of all kinds.

A jumping spider called *Mymarachne plataleoides* which lives in South-East Asia illustrates the cost of extreme specialization for fighting. All jumping spiders have sharp eyesight, and visual displays play an important role in reproduction. Accordingly, they have evolved elaborate features around their faces and mouth parts which, in this species, are taken to extremes. *Mymarachne* is a spider in ant's clothing! The immatures and females are almost identical, mimicking the ants among which they live and upon which they feed. However, during their last moult, the mature males undergo a dramatic metamorphosis, developing grotesque jaws and a pair of long, curving sabres. These are so out of proportion with the rest of the spider's body that they completely deform its appearance. Accounting for over two-thirds of the spider's length, the weapons are the most exaggerated emblems of masculinity in the animal kingdom. For much of the time they are folded, but they spring apart when the males challenge each other. The contestants face each other with outstretched jaws and fangs at the ready. The encounters involve a lot of sparring and fencing, with the males pushing and shoving against each other until one gives way, the advantage generally going to the fighter displaying the widest spanning jaws.

Although such specimens are likely to mate, their long-term prospects for survival are not good. Unfortunately, their transformation into warriors is so complete that their accoutrements greatly impede their ability to consume food; their fangs are simply too cumbersome to inject venom into their prey.

Flashy fighters

Outright aggression pays dividends for those who win, because the champions enjoy a period, albeit brief, in which they have opportunities to copulate with several females. But the stakes are high and the inevitable costs of combat take their toll. It is therefore not surprising to discover that the males of some species compete equally seriously without coming into damaging contact with each other.

Being macho is only one of three basic methods in which males obtain mates. The males of many kinds of creatures from across the animal kingdom have opted to display their superior quality through glamour rather than sheer aggression. But being beautiful is no soft option in the mating stakes. The intensity of the competition between foppish males is no less fierce, and each one's determination to win well is just as powerful as it is among males which have taken the route of armed combat.

The flashy patterns and coloration of their bodies generally add impact to their sexual displays and so make them more alluring to their more modestly attired partners. In fact, during the mating season, males behave rather like advertising hoardings, hard-selling themselves at the expense of their competitors – this is the subject of Chapter 2. But as well as exciting and enticing females, their courtship rituals often have another purpose – to intimidate and outshine rivals.

This is wonderfully exemplified by many birds. For sheer magnificence, the male mandarin duck, resplendent in plumage which includes patches of glossy green, coppery red, steel blue, orange, velvet black and maroon, rivals the very best of the birds of paradise. Intense competition among the drakes is probably responsible for the evolution of these gorgeous feathers. Considered for centuries as symbols of conjugal fidelity by the Japanese and Chinese, in reality mandarins are quite promiscuous. During early spring the drakes gather in groups for prolonged periods of competitive displaying. They often seem indifferent to the presence of any drab females, but instead direct their rituals towards each other. With crests raised, hackles spread and sail-like wing feathers erected, the drakes manoeuvre around each other while performing exaggerated body shakes, head dipping and mock wing preening, occasionally lifting their orange sails to expose iridescent inner wing feathers. This colourful posturing is clearly designed to sort out the males' ranking order and perhaps impress the females as to their relative fitness for mating. At other times, the drakes cluster around the females, displaying all the while, and wait for them to make their choice. Once mated, the female leaves to incubate her eggs and care for the ducklings by herself.

The use of fine feathers in fighting and pulling rank can be witnessed in birds such as ruffs and black grouse, which gather in communal arenas to display and mate. In full breeding dress a cock black grouse is an impressive creature with a lyre-shaped tail, black plumage shot with iridescence, a scarlet wattle above his eye and dazzling white under-tail coverts. In northern Europe, where most of these birds live, the cocks assemble in their arenas just before dawn and in the dim light re-establish their small territories and pecking orders with much frenetic activity and calling. Often well before any hens arrive, the cocks strike up a chorus of 'rookooing' calls, strut towards each other, heads bowing, necks swollen, wings trailing and tails fully fanned, thus making themselves look as impressive as possible. Neighbouring birds frequently engage in ritualized duels at the edges of their territories in a flurry of 'flutter jumping' and hissing. Sometimes they cling to each other and strike out with their beaks. The activity soon subsides as individual statuses within the arena are re-established, only to resume in bouts of urgent showing off with the arrival of hens, which mate chiefly with the dominant male. An hour or two after sunrise, the birds disperse for the rest of the day, to resume their courting in the early hours of the following morning.

Cock Australasian satin bowerbirds are flashy creatures, but they have an added trick to sabotage their hated rivals. The metallic blue males with their beady sapphire eyes build avenues of sticks on the rain-forest floors. Each cock strives to make his bower, strewn with blue berries and rosella feathers, more attractive to hens than his neighbours'. By the riveting nature of his courtship dance and the well-placed decorations, he entices females to enter between the rows of twigs, whereupon he mates with them. However, in areas where there is a high density of bowers, the hens are spoilt for choice. Desperation has turned each cock into an inveterate

thief, losing no opportunity to visit his neighbours' arenas and steal whatever takes his eye. Given the chance, a dominant male will demolish a rival's bower, using some of the sticks and colourful trophies to enhance his own construction and setting his neighbour back in the competition for mates. For a fuller description of these extraordinary bowers, see Chapter 2.

Sneaky males

Males can also secure sex by being sneaky. While the large warriors and dandies are preoccupied by their all-consuming battles and rituals, opportunities occasionally open up which can be seized by the less feisty males. Under these circumstances, being crafty can be immensely rewarding.

The problem for most males is that they must often wait on the side-lines, sometimes for years, until they are in a position to challenge the dominant breeders – and then most will fail. In the interim, they resort to sneaky tactics. In southern fur seals, the beachmasters are typical warriors and each stakes out

ABOVE Glamour boy! A cock red-capped manakin from the forests of Costa Rica outshines rivals and impresses hens with dazzling colours and fancy footwork.

RIGHT Shore of success: each warrior male fur seal holds a harem of thirty or more females on an Antarctic beach. But waiting just offshore, a line of sneaky males are ready to strike.

a territory which it defends violently from other males, creating the most vicious fights in the animal world. The bulls aim for the vulnerable soft skin around the fore flippers, ripping huge gashes in them with their teeth. The combatants sometimes end up with horrific injuries, such as torn muzzles, dislocated jaws, missing eyes and great chunks bitten out of their pelts. At this time, the bulls appear to be immune from pain; those which have commandeered prime positions on the beach rarely stand down and they valiantly stave off challenges from neighbouring males. Many pups are crushed in the resulting mayhem on the crowded rookeries. The beachmasters guard their precious freeholds for between eight and twelve weeks, during which time they fast and slowly lose condition. Other bulls lurk just offshore, getting thoroughly frustrated while feeding and watching for an opportunity to take on a weakened territory holder. At just the time when many of the cows are coming into season, these vigorous bulls charge ashore, toppling the dominant beachmasters when they are least able to defend themselves. The crafty males thus take over a harem of cows by sneaky tactics.

The use of the word 'sneaky' in this context might be taken to imply that the males are being unfair and somehow 'breaking the rules'. But far from it – this behaviour is an expression of pushiness, an essential quality of maleness, and is a counter to situations generated by superior individuals. Being 'sneaky' is about responding to opportunities and is a perfectly decent strategy if the lesser male succeeds in fathering some offspring. It is also highly likely that some sneaky males grow up to be the titans of their species. An elegant example of this 'wimp to warrior' strategy is provided by a fascinating cichlid fish which lives in Lake Tanganyika.

Several major lakes nestle in Africa's Great Rift Valley and, as lakes go, many of them are very ancient. Over millions of years of isolation, they have been centres of fast-track evolution, and the cichlid fish in lakes such as Malawi and Tangyanika have blossomed into about a thousand different species, each with its own way of making a living. There are algal scrapers, leaf choppers, scale eaters, shell crushers, diggers, hunters and plankton filterers; there is even one species that survives by biting out the eyes of other fish. Many are colourful and have remarkable breeding arrangements; in Lake Tanganyika, fifteen kinds employ empty water-snail shells as receptacles for their eggs, although one, called *Lamprologus callipterus*, is especially interesting. This shell-brooding cichlid holds the record for proportionately the largest males in the animal kingdom. The fully grown ones are giants, up to thirty times the size of their mates; in human terms, this is equivalent to the difference between an 80-kilogram (180-pound) man and the average newborn baby.

There is a good reason for this disparity between the sexes. The breeding males, resplendent in their black and yellow-rimmed fins, need to be big and powerful to defend territories on the sandy bottom around the edge of the lake and to be able to lift heavy snail shells. Each one assembles a hoard of a hundred or so in the centre of his territory, and is forever adding to his collection by stealing the shells of his neighbours which, in turn, steal from him. The females need to be small because they have to be able to fit inside the shells. When gravid, they move around inspecting the prized possessions of several males and, once satisfied that they have found a shell size sufficiently similar to their own for a snug fit, they enter the spiral chamber and spawn while the warrior male sheds his milt (sperm) over the entrance. For the next twelve days, the female lives inside the shell, guarding her eggs and fry until they are able to fend for themselves.

Obviously, the more shells a male can accumulate, the greater the number of females he can host and so the greater his breeding success. This is partly dependent upon his size, because he has to be big enough to fend off rival males and powerful enough to swim some distance carrying heavy shells in his mouth. By contrast, diminutive females are at an advantage because they can snuggle into water-snail shells where they can ensure protection for their offspring – but only if their nest remains with one male. If their shell is stolen and taken into a rival male's 'harem', they will be forced out into the open. It is not in the interests of the new male to protect a brood that has been conceived with the help of another male's sperm, so after he sets the occupied shell down, he smothers it with sand by a few powerful strokes of his tail. As the female faces suffocation, she quickly struggles free of her nursery and leaves it vacant for another female ready to spawn with the new male.

But the breeding business does not always run smoothly for the brawny males. At any given time, there are large numbers of young males as yet too small to defend their own stockpiles of shells but capable of fertilizing eggs. They assemble into marauding shoals and, at the first sign of spawning females, they invade the territories of the large males. Although the huge males try to keep their patch of sand free of them, they are completely overwhelmed by the sheer numbers of the smaller and more agile fish. While the territorial male is preoccupied in fending off the blitzkrieg, some of the young males manage to fertilize the freshly spawned eggs.

A few of the young males appear to lurk around the shells containing the females, and manage to deceive the 'shell master' by assuming female coloration, at least when he is looking! When the dominant male is otherwise occupied, the youngsters change back into courting colours and shed their own sperm into the occupied shells.

Housing the harem.
A male shell-brooding
cichlid is kept busy defending
his shells, inside which are
much smaller females
and their eggs. Thieves
and sneaky males are
a constant threat.

These young fish will eventually grow into giant males. However, this shell-brooding cichlid also has a quite different kind of male – seemingly a wimp if ever there was one. Only recently discovered by Japanese scientists, they are transvestite and resemble non-breeding females so that they can enter the territories of the large males with impunity. Without being hassled, they make for the occupied shells and wriggle past the females until they reach the innermost part of the chamber. Here they are at a considerable advantage over the larger male as they can secretly fertilize the female's eggs within the confines of the shell. Strange though it seems, these clandestine female-mimics never grow into big fish; yet they appear to be genetically similar to the large males, so something must happen during the course of their development to stunt their growth. Nevertheless, dwarf stature is a remarkable ploy evolved by some males to avoid competing for mates on equal terms with fierce warriors.

So 'wimps' can occasionally outwit warriors by behaving in an obsequious manner. This goes to show that, far from being merely 'punch drunk' pugilists, males vie with one another in a multitude of ways to achieve the sexual connection and, quite clearly, some manage to do so without being supreme fighters or flashy dancers. The extent of their success depends upon how many other males are competing in the same theatre of war and the blend of tactics which the adversaries employ.

This blend of tactics is easy to observe in the lichen-covered rock gardens of California. Here there is a population of lizards in which the males have evolved different coloured throat patches. These characterize classes of males, each of which employs different tactics for securing sex.

Like many lizards, side-blotched lizards wear their courting colours on their heads; some males have blue throats, others have a distinctly orange hue and the rest are yellow-throated. What makes this species so special is that these are colour codes for males adopting three sorts of tactics to obtain matings. The blue-throated

Colour-coded males

Side-blotched lizards: (below left) a blue-throated male makes a sexual conquest; (insets, from top) a supersexed roving orange-throated, a territorial blue-throated and a transvestite yellow-throated lizard.

males are quite similar to the closely related and commoner fence lizard. They are fairly pugnacious; each fights for his own territory, into which he will lure a female, mate with her and guard her assiduously from the attentions of trespassing suitors.

Settling down is not for the orange-throated specimens, which are super-charged, super-sexed and super-aggressive individuals, always on the move. They are so hyped up that they rarely live more than two years, whereas the steadier blue-throated males may survive for seven. Being utterly fearless, the fast-living orange-throated males invade the clusters of rocks commandeered by the blue throats, challenge and invariably thrash them. Any female present generally falls for the victor's vigorous wooing and submits to a sexual embrace. If it was not for the presence of a third type of male, the orange-throated ones would outbreed the pedestrian blue-throated ones. However, the members of this category, the yellow-throated males, resemble females and, lacking the specific colours of both kinds of warrior lizards, are not recognized as a threat by either of them. When they are engaged in fighting, or when a blue-throated male's back is turned, the 'transvestite' male sneaks into the territories and seizes his chance with any female. The sneaky yellow males therefore prevent the polygamous orange-throated males from becoming too successful.

There is a further complication which has a bearing upon the co-existence of males with three mating strategies. The mystery was solved by watching the behaviour of a fast-moving predatory snake aptly named the coach whip. This leather-brown serpent slithers around the rocks, occasionally elevating the front of its body like a snorkel to peer over the rocks. It seems that the territorial side-blotched lizards are vulnerable to the attentions of coach-whip snakes and in some years, perhaps when the snake population is high, coach-whips almost wipe out the males in fixed territories – the blue throats – thus benefiting the roving yellow- and orange-throated males. So there must be a balance of advantages and disadvantages to each of the different kinds of males, and the proportion of each will swing backwards and forwards from one year to another.

Gender jumpers

So the warriors and dandies of the natural world may gain mates through brute force or low cunning. But so relentless is the drive to carry on their genetic line that the males of some species have evolved other quite astonishing ploys to maximize their breeding potential. One surprising technique is gender jumping. To switch sex seems to defy a very fundamental aspect of nature and yet, amazingly, some animals do it as a normal part of growing up. Many marine creatures which broadcast vast numbers of eggs, sperm or larvae into the open ocean start life as males and graduate to being females as they grow up. This makes evolutionary sense for such species, because the males do not usually guard or have to fight for females, so there is no advantage to them in being big. After all, small males can still produce billions of sperm. However, size is of reproductive advantage to females because the bigger they are, the more eggs they can produce. An individual which changes sex at the right size or age will therefore leave more offspring than one which remains exclusively male or female.

For this reason, many marine molluscs such as oysters start out as relatively small males and then alter their gender as they grow, sometimes passing through a hermaphrodite stage in the process. The fornicating slipper limpet is one such animal. Those which have beachcombed around the flat, muddy creeks of south-eastern England or the northern coasts of Holland and Germany will be familiar with their shells. They have a peculiar habit of living in chains, formed by one animal settling on the back of another, and then another settling on top of that, and so on, until eight or nine cling together like a pile of inverted teacups. The chains are the result of the limpet's unusual sexual requirements. As the young molluscs mature, they develop into males gripped by wanderlust. They crawl until they make contact with another slipper shell larger than themselves, which is almost bound to be older, with two sets of sex organs. Mounting the shell, the young male docks his large penis into the female port of the one beneath it. Eventually, the male starts to develop female organs as well; these will host the penis of the slipper limpet that settles on his shell. As it grows, the mollusc becomes fully female, with nothing left of 'her' male anatomy.

For many kinds of fish, gender jumping is a regular feature of life. For instance, clown fishes are rarely found more than a metre (3 feet) or so away from the corollas of large tropical sea anemones – and seem unaffected by their stinging cells when they snuggle down for protection among the tentacles. Clown fish society consists simply of a breeding pair together with a variable number of juveniles. Such a monogamous arrangement without much competition for mates favours small males which change into females as they grow larger. A wimpish male is sufficient to act as an effective sperm producer for his mate's eggs. Should the female vanish, the male puts on weight, changes gender and forms a breeding partnership with another small male.

By far the more usual direction for fishes to jump gender is from female to male. This strategy is adopted by the polygamous wrasses, groupers, parrot and angel fishes – all dazzling inhabitants of the coral gardens where sex takes all kinds of fascinating twists and turns. In these fish, young males would have no chance of

gathering and defending their own group of spawning females in the face of competition from the large, aggressive harem holders. It therefore pays young wrasses and the like to be female. No matter how small, they will at least be able to spawn. However, as each grows older and bulkier, then, given the chance, it is better for a female to change sex. As a male, it can now round up its own group of females and father all their offspring.

Aggression plays a key role in the life of a gender-jumping wrasse. Each territory contains a tyrannical male which firmly dominates his harem of six or more mates. Only by continually demonstrating his command over them can he prevent one of them from changing sex and usurping his position of power. When young, the small wrasse join the harems as spawning females at the bottom of the pecking order and, bearing the brunt of everyone's hostility, their masculine tendencies are suppressed. But as they grow, each has the potential to be a male. The chance to switch sex and status

OPPOSITE Ladies-in-waiting. When the purplish male wrasse dies (top right), the largest of his entourage of orange females will change sex and take charge.

BELOW Big and brawny, that's the female anemone fish (left). The wimpish male just supplies sperm. When she dies, he grows, jumps gender, and lays eggs.

31

comes with the death of the despotic male. Within an hour or two of his disappearance, the largest and most dominant female becomes aggressive and starts to behave like the departed 'master', chivvying the rest of the females and defending the area against neighbouring males. Should one of them beat her into submission, her transformation will be halted. If not, within about ten days or so, 'she' will be irrevocably changed to a fully functioning 'he' and produce active sperm.

The more closely the sex lives of fish are investigated, the more complex they turn out to be. For instance, there are two kinds of male blue-head wrasse. The species is a common inhabitant of the Caribbean reefs, feeding on zooplankton during the mornings and spawning during a two-hour period each afternoon throughout the year. Blue-heads' reproductive behaviour falls into two types; they spawn either in pairs or in groups in which one female is pursued by up to twenty or so males. However, the males involved in these two forms of spawning are quite different. Those which engage in group sex are the so-called primary males. Each develops directly into a male and is endowed with large testes capable of manufacturing vast quantities of sperm, all the better to compete with other males in the race to fertilize the eggs. And yet, curiously enough, these feisty fish resemble females in their size and hue, presumably so as not to provoke the territorial and distinctively coloured super-males. These begin life as egg-bearing females, but the largest among them can change sex and become colourful super-males. This happens if some of the existing dominant males are removed from the reef, either experimentally or naturally by predators such as barracuda. Within hours, the newly dominant females begin to exhibit super-male behaviour by courting and defending territories; after a week, their ovaries have changed into fully functional but comparatively small testes.

Sex changing – what's the catch?

If all animals could change their sex, would they do it? The answer is probably yes. There is an attraction in escaping the costs of fighting by starting out as a female and producing a limited number of eggs, then, when old enough and large enough, changing sex, winning male battles and making 'cheap' sperm by the billion in order to fertilize as many females as possible. It seems an enticing and highly viable way of producing the maximum number of offspring. However, although one kind of South African reed frog has been recorded changing sex, no genuine case of gender jumping has been found in reptiles, birds and mammals. Why should this be so? The reason must be something to do with the circumstances in which these animals find themselves.

As discussed in Chapter 3, the move out of water involved a more challenging lifestyle because surviving and breeding on the land forced animals to perfect insemination techniques and to package eggs in ever more complex ways to prevent them drying out. Commensurate with this particular development, females became anatomically more 'feminine', with special ducts and glands for putting waterproof shells on their eggs, and ultimately evolved uteruses in which their babies could begin their development. The increasing customization of females drove an even deeper wedge between them and their males, which became more competitive and structurally modified for combat and courtship.

These changes drove the sexes down an evolutionary road of no return. Convincing proof is revealed by comparing the insides of gender jumpers and sexually committed creatures. In fish such as wrasses, the only noticeable difference between the sexes is the presence of either testes or ovaries – and even these can look superficially the same. However, in a mammal such as a fox, the vixen sports not only ovaries, a uterus and mammary glands, but also a completely different arrangement of external genitalia from that of her mate. So perhaps the anatomical implications of a sexual refit may be too fundamental for gender swapping in such advanced creatures. For this reason, changing sex is impossible in our own species. Although it is always trumpeted in the press when some man or woman decides to have parts of his or her body refashioned in the likeness of the opposite sex, the 'change' effected by the surgeon's knife is merely cosmetic. For us and the majority of terrestrial creatures, gender is determined by our chromosomes and developmental biology, and is fixed for life.

OVERLEAF LEFT
A monstrous mistress or wimpish lover? In animals like the wood spider in which males do not battle for mates, the females are the larger sex. The bigger they are, the more eggs they produce.

OVERLEAF RIGHT
A life-long bond: a pair of tiny male deep-sea angler fish have become permanently fused to a female. They will fertilize her eggs on demand.

Small is sexy

In the vertebrates and insects, extreme sexual dimorphism – huge differences between the sexes – has come about because the males have evolved into weapon-bearing warriors designed for acquiring harems. However, in species in which males have opted for dedicated monogamy, the females are usually the larger sex; in some cases, the males are miniaturized. 'Dwarf' males are found in a variety of flatworms, nematodes, crustaceans and molluscs. In the oyster *Ostrea pulchrana*, the large females host the small males on their shells and may even retard their growth through some chemical influence. Charles Darwin was aware

of degenerate males when he studied barnacles. As adults, these are sedentary crustaceans which survive by straining planktonic food out of the sea and kicking it into their mouths. The only competition they experience is for dwelling space on the rocks which they encrust around the shores. Although they are mostly hermaphrodite, they cross-fertilize each other's eggs, each one extending a long, roving penis – relatively speaking, the longest in the world – to transport sperm to its neighbours. However, some barnacles are parasites, bearing little resemblance to crustaceans, and with separate sexes. The vanishingly small males enter their mates as free-swimming larvae and settle inside their partners' tissues, resembling alien parasites themselves! In the barnacle Trypetesa, which burrows into mollusc shells, the diminutive males are reduced to little more than their gonads, permanently lodged as sperm banks inside the females.

Even larger animals can live in circumstances in which they are highly scattered and the chances of meeting one another are slim. Once again, competition among males for mates will be rare and occasionally the evolutionary and ecological pressures are such that those which mature rapidly as dwarfs are at an advantage because they are in a position to settle down as soon as possible with any female they manage to locate and become their live-in lover. It is a strategy of 'first come, first served'.

The best-known example comes from the cold, dark depths of the ocean where about a hundred kinds of grotesque Ceratoid angler fish drift. They are the ultimate 'stealth' hunters. Each one attracts other fish and crustaceans to their doom by a luminous lure dangling above its malevolent-looking mouth. Up until the moment when the jaws snap shut, the dazzled prey suspects nothing, because the angler's velvet-black body fails to reflect any glimmer of light – even from the lure – to give away its presence. Some species of angler have virtually transparent bodies for the same reason.

For a long time after their discovery, the details of the deep-sea angler's sex life remained a mystery; it was widely held that they must have dispensed with sex, because those trawled up from the abyssal depths were always females. The first clue that something unusual was going on came to light in 1922, when an Icelandic marine scientist looked carefully at two tiny fish that were attached by their snouts to the belly of a female deep-sea angler. He thought that they were young ones, although he was at a loss to understand how they had become fastened to the female. The truth dawned three years later when another ichthyologist dissected a fleshy growth on the body of another female and found it to be a 'parasitic' male.

Initially, the male deep-sea anglers are free-swimming, but they could easily be mistaken for a quite different species. They have one role in life – to find a mate.

All their internal organs are rudimentary except the testes, but to help them in their mission they are equipped with large nostrils, presumably for locating females by their sexual underwater scent, and sharp pincer-like teeth for clamping securely on to their prospective partner. In some species, once the tiny male has made contact with his mate, he bonds with her for life. His body merges with hers, even sharing her blood supply, because once the male is *in situ* he depends utterly upon his ogreish mate for nourishment. In the end, the male is reduced to a fleshy appendage, a blob of testis under the complete control of the gravid female. When the host is ready to spawn she synchronizes the release of a cloud of sperm by hormones circulating in her blood.

Perhaps the most bizarre example of a dwindling male is found in an unusual-looking marine worm called *Bonellia*. It has a sedentary lifestyle and often resides in the galleries and ducts formed by boring molluscs around the rocky shores of the Mediterranean and the Pacific North-West. These worms start life as free swimming larvae, and whether they turn into a male or female depends upon the kind of environment they encounter. A larva that settles somewhere that is unoccupied by other worms grows into a female with an acorn-sized body from which extends a mobile proboscis for hoovering up detritus. It is capable of enormous elongation, and when fully stretched may be over 1 metre (3 feet) long. On the other hand, a larva that detects the presence of a female attaches itself to her body by means of a muscular sucker. Most of its organ systems either fail to develop or degenerate. After a week, the diminutive, stunted male – barely a centimetre or two (less than an inch) long – becomes mobile, makes his way through his gargantuan mate's gut and takes up a prime position for fertilizing her eggs close to her oviduct, where he remains as a live-in testis, leaking sperm.

This incredible arrangement is not solely for the benefit of the female. It is a male tactic that works best when potential mates are well dispersed and encountering them is rare. Under these circumstances, being large and pugnacious will not help a male to acquire more mates. A male which is able to find a female and stick to her wins the day by fathering her offspring.

But for most kinds of animals, no matter what tactics the males employ to further their sexual aspirations, it is the females which determine the winners. This is because – as we shall see in the next chapter – it is they which do the choosing.

CHAPTER

2

CHOOSY
FEMALES

Although females behave less dramatically than males, they have a very crucial hand to play in the mating game. They are not, as usually portrayed, passive recipients of male lust, but are naturally cautious and highly discriminating when deciding with which to copulate. From their point of view, all males are different and, as every female wants only the very best possible specimen to father her offspring, she plays for time while assessing the quality of what is on offer. Females therefore go shopping for sex and males must market themselves like animated billboards to attract a customer. Lavish ornamentation often means quality, because mediocre males cannot afford the luxury of 'expensive' displays. By weighing up the choice of mates and choosing only the chirpiest or flashiest partners, females act as wildly imaginative artists, capable of 'creating', through sexual selection, males which are as breathtakingly gorgeous as they are bizarre.

PREVIOUS PAGES
Who's a pretty boy?
Female Raggiana birds of
paradise assess the quality
of a displaying male in the
jungle of Papua New Guinea.
But is he splendid enough
for them to fall for him?

Like male competition, female fussiness can be explained by the profound reproductive differences between the sexes. As discussed in Chapter 1, with the expenditure of only a little semen, males can generate an almost unlimited number of offspring by being promiscuous, while females bear higher reproductive costs by producing big eggs or supporting long pregnancies. They are therefore not so fecund.

This asymmetry is easy to appreciate in species such as guillemots. Resembling penguins with wings, these auks crowd on to remote cliffs and rocky stacks in northern latitudes in order to breed. During spring, the colonies bustle with courting birds, and promiscuous coupling is much in evidence. Each hen lays a single pear-shaped egg that will be replaced only if the first one is accidentally knocked off the ledge or devoured by gulls. In any event, only one egg can be balanced on top of the female's legs and incubated against a patch of bare skin under the fold of her belly. Being relatively large, the egg represents not only a considerable investment of the hen's resources, but also her sole chance that year of raising a chick. Given a choice, she is therefore very careful about which male will fertilize her precious possession. She is on the look-out for the best father for her single chick – a healthy, assertive male which can demonstrate his prowess at catching fish through courtship feeding. A good provider will presumably pass on these qualities to her offspring, thus ensuring its long-term survival.

The difference in investment is just as marked in creatures whose females produce a whole basket of eggs. Green turtles migrate vast distances across the oceans from their feeding grounds to tropical islands where they seek sand, sun and sex. The mature males wait offshore to intercept the gravid females as they head for the beach and, with the assistance of a pair of claws on their front flippers, cling to their mates' shells and copulate with them. Once inseminated, each female continues her journey, breaking through the surf usually at night to drag herself on to the sand. Beyond the highest tidemark, she digs a hole in which she deposits a clutch of about 100 eggs, each one about the size and shape of a ping-pong ball. After about ten minutes, the spent female fills in the nest and retreats laboriously back to the sea. Nevertheless, during the space of a few weeks, she'll be back to repeat the process up to five times, leaving about 500 eggs to be incubated by the heat of the sun. Female turtles find this an exhausting business: it takes them three years of grazing on 'turtle grass' to lay up sufficient reserves to make another sea-trek back to the breeding beaches.

By contrast, a dominant male green turtle's contribution is minimal – perhaps a teaspoonful of semen every time he mates. Furthermore, he can latch on to several females in succession, fathering thousands of hatchlings in the process, and be ready to mate every year.

In order to stand a chance of breeding, males must catch the eye of females and impress them, and across the animal kingdom males have exploited all possible ways of showing off. Sometimes the surroundings or the lifestyle of the creatures deter-mines the medium males employ to boast about themselves. For instance, birds which live in thickly vegetated places such as reed-beds or which are active under the cover of darkness use sound – bitterns 'boom' like foghorns, reed warblers utter a seamless stream of musical phrases, owls hoot and nightjars churr continuously. Those which advertise on the open plains – where it is easier to see over great distances – often signal by erecting conspicuous plumage. Most birds use a combi-nation of both visual and vocal displays when attempting to sell themselves to prospective mates.

Among the amphibians, male frogs woo by trilling or croaking. Male anolid lizards erect brightly coloured dewlaps, while fish tend to flourish decorative fins. Most mammals have keen noses and accordingly use seductive odours to meet up with the opposite sex. Some insects stridulate – make a chirping or scraping sound, like grasshoppers – for sex, whereas others deploy potent scent to lure mates – emperor moths can home in from 3 kilometres (2 miles) away by following a plume of perfume which acts as both an irresistible attractant and an aphrodisiac to members of the opposite sex; in web-building spiders, the males strum a tattoo on the silken threads which their partners perceive through their feet. Fireflies emit

LEFT Driven to extremes. The shimmering glory of the peacock evolved because females have always fallen for the flashiest males. This finery must be a reflection of good genes.

RIGHT A precious bundle. A female guillemot's one and only egg for the year means she must be very choosy about the father. But the male can play the field.

flashes of light, certain diurnal butterflies reflect patterns of ultra-violet and electric fish communicate with each other in the murky waters where they live by discharging pulses of electrical energy.

In some species, the males advertise for sex in such an extravagant manner as to defy our imagination – and all because they must catch the eye of a discerning female.

The blue peafowl is the largest and most spectacular of the true pheasants. In full courtship mode the male is, without a doubt, one of the wonders of nature and an eloquent testament to the creative force of sexual selection. Indeed, it is

Flash fathers make fitter offspring

such an improbable creature that, were peacocks not to exist, we could surely never have envisaged one. This legendary creature has been fashioned over countless generations by peahens choosing males with the most gorgeous rear ends to father their chicks.

The male is nothing less than an ostentatious sexual advertisement, proclaiming with strident voice and ornate plumage that he is the best source of sperm. Designed to be seen by the hen from the front, his display begins with him lifting and spreading his train; it forms an enormous fan, decorated with serried ranks of beautifully iridescent eye-spots, framing his glossy blue neck and underparts. The impact of the performance is enhanced when he rustles the feathers in his train so that the metallic eye-spots shimmer, suggesting a great deal more movement than is actually happening. Each eye-spot is like a miniature icon of the bird itself, mirroring the eye-catching blues and greens of the body plumage. It is as though the peacock were the star on his own stage, surrounded by a chorus line of tiny males scintillating with every vibration of his fan. If the show is a hit, the peahen to which it is directed appears mesmerized and the male is allowed to mount her.

There is something deeply puzzling about the peacock's 'tail' – it is fundamentally a useless appendage, both an impediment to flight and a drain on the male's resources. And yet it is readily apparent that peacocks with the more visually arresting displays are the hottest in attracting customers – the longer the trains, the more the peahens fall for them. Not that peahens have a fetish for flashy tails *per se*, but being energetically costly adornments to grow and maintain, they are a true indication of the cock's vigour and social status. A dazzling tail could never be 'afforded' by a mediocre or unhealthy male, which therefore stands no chance of seducing females. Peahens certainly recognize a good male because, given a choice, they are unanimous in submitting to the same individual. What seems to impress them is the number and quality of the eye-spots, which increase with the age of the male. As longevity may reflect a male's sturdy constitution, females may fall for traits that demonstrate their partner's enduring qualities on the basis that these will be transmitted to their offspring.

But sex is not the end of this affair. Peahens are remarkably possessive of the peacock with which they have mated and, although they need to be inseminated only once to have their eggs fertilized, each female tries to monopolize his attentions by being aggressive to other hens or by actively soliciting further copulations from the male if he starts to court another. By exhausting the male's supply of sperm, the peahen attempts to prevent him passing on his desirable characteristics to the offspring of other peahens, which will inevitably compete with her own.

Bridal bowers

Some of the most extraordinary birds to be seen in Australia and New Guinea are the dozen or so bowerbirds which rate as the landscape artists of the avian world. The fact that most native mammalian predators in Australasia are nocturnal makes it possible for the males to spend the days displaying on courts close to or on the ground, which they meticulously prepare for the purpose of sex and seduction. As they eschew parental duties and the forest provides plenty of easily obtained food, the males are able to dedicate much of their year to building and decorating their bowers. The hens behave like connoisseurs of art, awarding their sexual favours to the owners whose works impress them most. Depending upon the species, the male bowerbirds build structures ranging from simple avenues of twigs – like the dazzling yellow and black regent bowerbird's – to more elaborate ones which the owners embellish with all manner of bright objects; the cock satin bowerbird even daubs the walls of his bower with 'paint' derived from strongly coloured berries crushed in his beak.

But these are as nothing compared to the achievements of three gardener bowerbirds – Macgregor's, the striped and the Vogelkop – which practise their art deep in the forests of New Guinea. These mostly brown birds, the size of a starling, are master builders, constructing out of interlocking twigs maypole-like towers up to 3 metres (10 feet) in height, and huts resembling tepees supported by internal columns with passageways connecting inner chambers. Furthermore, the birds landscape their buildings with carefully tended forecourts on which all kinds of eye-catching treasures are displayed. In the case of Macgregor's bowerbirds, and possibly the others, decorative fruit is brought into the bower and the cache doubles up as a snack bar, allowing the cock bird to spend more time on site advertising for hens.

Although they all construct amazing bowers, Vogelkop bowerbirds – from the mountains on the western tip of Irian Jaya – produce the most extravagant exhibitions of landscape art. The male's arena is 5–6 metres (16–20 feet) across, with his astonishing bower in the centre. This is constructed around a sapling and is completely covered in by a thatched roof which is supported internally by several pillars. In front of the entrance is the garden, on which is meticulously arranged a variety of pretty or conspicuous objects gathered from the surrounding forest – a number of faded yellow leaves laid out in a pattern, a heap of brightly coloured berries, the iridescent wing-cases of a certain kind of beetle and fresh flowers which are changed daily before they wilt. The industry involved in maintaining such an arena must be phenomenal and yet the investment will be well worth while if the hens are impressed and allow the male to father their next broods.

What countless generations of hen bowerbirds have been doing is giving their sexual vote to cocks with the most colourful courts, rather than to those with the most colourful plumes. Indeed, as the features that the hens found seductive were transferred from the body to the bower, the males seem to have evolved camou-flage plumage. The male Vogelkop is the plainest of the gardeners, with no hint of the orange crest sported by the closely related Macgregor's and striped bowerbirds. With such a stunning display in his bower, the Vogelkop has relinquished the need for bright feathers. The advantage to the male is clear: the adornments in his garden

Bridal bower. The male Vogelkop bowerbird designs his own garden for sex and seduction. The fastidious females will judge his creation, and stay to mate if it is good enough.

are better than feathers. A male which depends on his fine plumage to attract a mate cannot change the shape and colour of his feathers – he is stuck with what he is born with. But a male bowerbird has a choice. If he fails to impress any hens with the layout of his bower, he can quickly alter the details – perhaps changing the flower arrangement on his forecourt or the position of the berries. In fact, male bowerbirds are forever fiddling about with the layout of their wares – removing a shrivelled fruit, shifting the position of a leaf or adding a bleached shell to the display. Sooner or later, a male might hit upon an arrangement that the hens find irresistible. If not, they will take their custom to one with a more pleasing exhibition.

Orange is best. The more brilliant a male guppy's orange fins, the better he is at finding food. The female will choose such a mate, so her offspring inherit his robust genes.

Females of other kinds of animals are smitten by quite different qualities in their mates, as a few examples will illustrate.

Different qualities matter to different species

When choosing sexual partners, females are often judging males for various strengths, and what they find 'sexy' depends upon the species to which they belong and the nature of their breeding arrangements. For instance, female guppies are impressed by males with deep orange fins and spots on their body. Originally, these hardy favourites of the aquarist trade were called 'millions fish' because myriads of them swim among the decaying vegetation and twisted roots at the edges of mangrove swamps in the Caribbean islands of Trinidad, Barbados and St Lucia, as well as in the adjacent regions of South America. Guppies are incessantly sexual and, as the females brood their eggs inside their bodies, they need to be fertilized internally by the males.

This happens by way of a tricky manoeuvre during which the male transfers sperm into his mate by means of his mobile anal fin, which is folded into a tube. To achieve such intimacy, the partners must be nicely co-ordinated, and this is achieved by an elaborate courtship performed by the males. Barely a thumb's length when fully mature, they are only half the size of the silvery females. And yet they are ostentatious little rakes, flaunting their ample fins, which are decorated with all the colours of the rainbow. However, the female guppies, ever on the look-out for a mate which stands out in the crowd, have an eye for males with especially bright splashes of orange on the fins. This is not simply a matter of taste – the intensity of the colour betrays another characteristic that the female seeks for her offspring. As the pigment is acquired in the food that the male eats, the depth of the coloraton is a measure of his skill as a hunter. A male guppy with patches of rich orange on his fins is therefore advertising the fact that he is an accomplished survivor and, if his success is dependent upon inherited qualities, they are precisely what the female wants her offspring to possess. She will therefore choose such males to fertilize her eggs and reject equally ardent suitors showing less orange on their bodies.

So females often need practical proof of a male's virtues and, in turn, the male needs to persuade a prospective mate that he has more to offer than any of his rivals. This may take the form of presenting the female with a prenuptial gift of food. The male wolf spider (*Pisaura mirabilis*), a common European species found hunting on the ground, catches a fly, trusses the corpse up in a dense wrapping of silk and offers it to the much larger and fearsome female. Although the silk may well be impregnated with chemicals that serve as an identification badge, the nutritional value of the fly is significant because well-fed females grow larger, lay more eggs and produce their egg batches more quickly after insemination than leaner specimens. Furthermore, large female wolf spiders live longer than poorly nourished ones and so eventually produce more spiderlings. Thus the gift of food is not bribery in return for copulation – it is in the male's interest to help fatten up his formidable mate.

As lack of food often restricts a female's capacity to manufacture eggs, it pays her to opt for a male bearing the best edible gifts. Among the insects, male scorpion and hanging flies go courting carrying food. In the case of hanging flies, the female will yield only to a male which offers a sufficiently large fly for her to suck during the act of copulation. The larger the item of food, the longer the male is allowed to mate and the more eggs he manages to fertilize.

In bush crickets, the female receives an unusual but nevertheless important snack along with the sperm. The male delivers his semen in a parcel or spermatophore (see Chapter 3) which sometimes accounts for just over a quarter of his body weight. The terminal portion – called the spermatophylax – is mostly protein and, as it remains outside the female's vent after she has mated, she contorts her body and consumes it. This 'free' nourishment helps her to form more and better provisioned eggs. Predictably, female bush crickets show a decided preference for big males because they donate large spermatophores containing significantly more to eat than the packages of punier partners.

For a long time it was thought that 'courtship feeding' in birds was a purely symbolic activity that helped to maintain the pair bond. However, it now seems that the males are providing the hens with the extra food they need for egg formation and incubation. For instance, in highly active insectivorous species such as blue and great tits, the female can only just find sufficient food to maintain her own weight, and so it is the 'free' insects and caterpillars ferried to her by her partner that are processed into a clutch of eggs. Male European bee-eaters are generous in proffering insects caught on the wing to their partners, to the extent of giving away the larger items and swallowing the smaller insects themselves. However, in some birds there is more to 'courtship feeding' because the male plays a vitally important role in rearing the youngsters. So the female needs to select a cock bird which can convince her of his prowess as a tireless provider of food before she commits herself to him. Courtship feeding is therefore a test of a male's potential as a parent.

Female terns beg to be fed and the frequency of the male's response is seen as a measure of his parenting ability. Like all terns, Arctic terns are lovely, graceful seabirds, and at the beginning of the breeding season the males advertise for a mate by wheeling over the colonial nest sites on buoyant wings. Each of the screaming birds carries a freshly caught fish in his blood-red bill and hopes to attract the attention of unmated females. However, a male does not easily part with his hard earned gifts until he has secured the serious interest of a female, and then both sexes spend much of the time together on the feeding grounds. Here, the male is continuously pestered by his clamorous partner to give her a good proportion of his catch. What she might be judging is the frequency with which he returns to her with a silvery gift dangling from his beak. During the final phase of courtship, the female spends most of her time on the pair's territory, laying and looking after the clutch, so the male's capacity for catching fish is put to the test as he commutes to and from the fishing grounds to feed his mate.

The male is especially important during the period just after hatching, when the hen is brooding day and night and the male must once again be the sole provider of fish or shrimps. Most hens lay three eggs and in a good year a pair of terns can successfully fledge the first two to hatch. But the fate of the third usually hangs in the balance. Whether the chick survives or not depends upon the size of the egg from which it emerged and how hard the father works feeding the family. The prospects are better if the young tern hatches from a relatively large egg – which is a reflection of how well the female was fed by her partner during courtship – and if the male maintains a relentless supply of fish when the family arrives. Apparently, the two are related – a male Arctic tern which keeps his hen well provisioned during the egg-laying stage is likely to be an excellent provider later in the season. Many tern couples split up early in the courtship period, possibly because the female has weighed up her mate's performance and rejected a poor provider.

RIGHT The more a male Arctic tern courtship feeds, the more likely he is to become a hard-working father.

LEFT The way to a female's heart is through her stomach! A male sage bush cricket offers his wing cases as a sexual snack; a female bush cricket (inset) eating spermatophore donated by the male during mating.

Fat emus make better fathers

With the ability to look a man straight in the eye, the Australian emu is the second tallest bird in the world, surpassed only by the ostrich. It is also one of a select group in which the females take the initiative in courtship and relegate the role of parenting entirely to the males. The 'she-mu' therefore has much to lose if she trusts her eggs to the wrong mate, so her behaviour is designed to ensure that she makes no mistakes!

Although emus are widely distributed in Australia, they are best known as inhabitants of the arid mulga country on the east side of the continent, where they roam in small mobs. These scrublands are one of the main breeding grounds for these hefty, flightless birds whose unusual winter breeding and reversed sexual roles are well suited to the climate and the difficult environment in which they live. Tipping the scales at 35 kilograms (80 pounds), the female is generally the heavier of the sexes and, as the nesting season approaches, she develops nuptial coloration, with black neck feathers framing the small area of dark blue bare skin on the head and neck. The male's plumage does not darken, because his neck feathers remain small and the pale blue underlying skin shows through.

When she is ready to mate, the female calls the 'he-mus' in. She selects a spot close to her intended nest site, inflates her internal air sacs so that her neck swells causing the feathers to ruffle and, bowing forwards, delivers a series of deep, resonant booms not unlike the sound produced by a didgeridoo. Her song carries some distance and soon every male within earshot gravitates towards her. In the case of the female emu, it is certainly not a matter of 'first come, first served' – by calling them in, she encourages the males to compete among themselves for her favours, leaving the most dominant – and therefore the best – for her consideration. But she still has to weigh up whether the winner is good enough. What she is looking for is a plump partner. She may squat coyly and allow the male to mount but not initially to mate with her. It is thought that she is assessing his weight, and for a very good reason. If the male is an acceptable size, she allows him to insert his surprisingly long red penis and inseminate her.

The male's weight is crucial because he alone looks after the nest. The female produces a clutch of up to ten dark olive eggs, each weighing about 580 grams (21 ounces), which probably leaves her exhausted and in need of replenishing her depleted reserves. By leaving the male to hatch the eggs, she can devote her time to recuperating. He, by contrast, has to sit tight for about two months to protect their joint investment and keep the eggs warm until the chicks appear. This is no mean feat – in some areas, the nights are so cold that sunrise finds him with frost covering his back. To complete his task, the male emu must be well endowed with his own reserves of fat, because he rarely feeds during this period and by the time he has a young family to guard he has generally lost up to 10 kilograms (22 pounds) in weight. It is for this reason that female emus fall for fat males – lean ones would not be able to stay the course and would abandon the eggs to save themselves from starving.

The same probably holds true of polyandrous species, such as jacanas and moorhens. In the latter species, females are once again the larger sex; they too prefer to mate with cock birds which appear well filled out, because all the family duties fall on the males, from incubating the eggs through to caring for the chicks. A male well bolstered with fat may be a better bet as a potential father than a less well-provisioned one.

Sex and symmetry

Teasing apart, the ingredients of sex appeal is something of a challenge, but it is reasonable to suppose that a perfectly constructed symmetrical body, itself a consequence of problem-free development due in part at least to good genes, might be one of the elements of beauty. Scorpion-flies were the first animals to reveal that body symmetry may be important in mate selection. The discovery was made by Randy Thornhill of the University of New Mexico, Albuquerque, who demonstrated that females fell for males with nicely balanced wings. In fact, the choice was based upon the male's body odour (or pheromones), which was more seductive in symmetrical suitors than in the slightly lop-sided ones.

Since then, the association between sex appeal and symmetry has been discovered in several other kinds of animals. In fact, symmetry has even been invoked as part of the modern interpretation of the peacock's amazing train. Although parasites and the diseases they cause occasionally kill, they exert an especially strong influence early in life, causing deviations in the host's development. Such abnormalities may not be corrected and will be carried into adulthood as, for example, a slightly deformed body or a badly configured tail. A peahen wants only the fittest male to sire her offspring, so that he can transmit his robust constitution to her chicks, and it seems that she can assess whether or not a mature suitor has a scrofulous history by the magnificence of his train. This approach appears to work, because peacocks with symmetrical arrays of large eye-spots tend to sire chicks which are healthier and grow faster than those fathered by less impressive, flawed males.

Bilateral symmetry is fundamental to much of animal design – it has even been implicated as an element of beauty in our own bodies – but the sex appeal of symmetry has been quantified in swallows. The male swallow's chances of finding a mate are ruined if one of his tail streamers is much shorter than the other.

For us, the sexes of swallows are difficult to tell apart. However, a male is distinguished by his slightly longer outer tail feathers – a fifth longer than those of the females. These are shown off during courtship when, calling excitedly, he hovers around the female with his tail fully fanned. Working in rural Denmark, Anders Møller lengthened and shortened the tail feathers of male swallows with the help of scissors and superglue, and discovered that those with the longest tails were quickly snapped up by the hens as soon as they arrived around the barns and other farm buildings where they nested. Prompt pair formation means that there is time for the early nesters to go on and rear second broods. Less well-endowed males mated later and thus managed to raise only a single family during the summer. For male swallows there is therefore a clear reproductive benefit in possessing a long, forked tail. However, by artificially lengthening the streamers on some cock birds, Moller found that there was an optimum size beyond which they became an aerodynamic drag and jeopardized the male's ability to manoeuvre when foraging for insects.

Møller went on to discover the significance to the hens of long, attenuated tails. He tested the theory that they might be an indication of the male's inborn resistance to parasitic infections. Swallows, both adults and nestlings, commonly become infested with blood-sucking mites. These can breed so fast – 14,000 were estimated to live in one nest – that they can debilitate their hosts through either the blood they withdraw or diseases they transmit. If they survive at all, swallows reared in such heavily infested nests grow into comparatively small and underweight adults. However, the offspring of some pairs of swallows cope significantly better with the parasites than others. By swapping chicks between nests, Møller found that the differences in resistance to parasitic infections seemed to be partly inherited. Furthermore, nestlings fathered by males with the longest outer tail feathers had the smallest parasite loads, even if they were fostered in nests with big infestations of mites.

Møller concluded that the length and symmetry of the male's tail signals his ability to resist parasites or infectious microbial diseases. By letting such a male inseminate her, the female is unwittingly selecting his superior genes to pass on to their joint offspring.

These fascinating discoveries beg the question of how female barn swallows are able to tell the tails apart? Like many birds which intercept small insects, swallows have high-resolution vision. Many of the photo-sensitive cells – or cones – which line the backs of their eyes are furnished with red or yellow droplets of oil; these filter out the ultra-violet and blue wavelengths before the light penetrates the retina. Although their precise function is not fully understood, these pigmented globules may behave like internal sunglasses. By screening out the blue end of the spectrum, they possibly enhance the contrast within the visual field, making tiny insects stand out against the bright sky. Besides assisting the birds to detect their prey, such keen eyesight would also enable female swallows to resolve the image of the streamers on a distant male, and so assess his 'sexiness' by their length.

Dazzling duets

Scientists working in the sweltering forests of Costa Rica claim to have discovered that female long-tailed manakins may be the fussiest females in the animal kingdom. Cock long-tailed manakins are forced to be really high-pressure salesmen; they will be chosen to mate on the basis of how well they sing in tune, shine on the dance floor and excel themselves in an extraordinary test of stamina.

The fussiest of females. A hen long-tailed manakin (left) is so difficult to please that she demands to be entertained by teams of two males. Very few males ever manage to mate.

These sparrow-sized birds belong to a family of forty or so exotic species which are confined mostly to South America. Second only to the incomparable humming-birds, male manakins are dazzling feathered jewels, their plumage sparkling with sky blues, brilliant reds and yellows set against the deepest velvet black. Some of their wing and tail feathers are modified for producing a variety of instrumental sounds which supplement the curious vocalizations the male utters to draw the attention of the hens. The courtship displays are nothing short of virtuoso

performances, choreographed into series of pivoting movements, mincing steps, jumps, somersaults and butterfly flights. Although the details vary from species to species, the acrobatic displays of the manakins rival those of any bird of paradise and are equally difficult to observe because they take place either in the forest canopy or in deep cover near ground level.

The courtship of the long-tailed manakin is very curious indeed because the brightly coloured cocks form long-standing partnerships in which one bird is clearly senior to the other. And yet teamwork of the highest order is required in order to woo the dull green hens. Unlike the females, which shoulder the full responsibility for rearing the chicks, the cocks devote their lives to feeding and philandering – although in fact very few of them manage to father any offspring, and those which do almost dance themselves into their graves!

When a hen is ready to breed, she inspects all the brightly coloured males in her neighbourhood by visiting their display sites. She assesses each pair of males on their own stage, which usually consists of a thin horizontal branch stripped of leaves a metre (yard) or two above the forest floor. She finds them by homing in on the cock bird's incessant duetting. This is a melodious 'to-le-do' and is repeated up to a thousand times in an hour until a hen comes by to investigate. The hens must have a good ear for music, because they visit most frequently those pairs of males which sing most accurately in tune. Apparently, singers improve with practice, as the subordinate cock learns to match the pitch of his voice to that of his senior partner, so that the pair come to sing in perfect unison. If the hen likes what she hears, the threesome descend to the stage, where the cocks launch themselves into an amazing series of gymnastics, leap-frogging backwards over one another as they shuffle towards the female; they alternate this with taking it in turns to hover over each other and showing off the electric blue feathers on their backs.

This display may continue without interruption for twenty minutes and is clearly a test of the male's robust good health. In touring many stages and assessing as many as eighty males, the hen will have witnessed many dances below par – at least in her eyes. But when, finally, she discovers a performance to her liking, she indicates her willingness to copulate. However, this strenuous teamwork pays off handsomely only for the senior partner. From the hen's point of view, this handsome manakin is probably the best on offer, having repeatedly proved himself with one of the most physically demanding shows in the neighbourhood. Once she has made her choice, the top male signals his junior partner to make himself scarce. He then performs a solo dance in front of his admirer and then, in a flash, mounts and inseminates her. The reward for the junior male may come later – he may inherit the stage when the more experienced bird dies or vanishes, but he may have a long time to wait, because long-tailed manakins live for about fifteen years.

Almost all the hen manakins end up mating with but a handful of males. In one area with about eighty cocks, just five of them accounted for over 90 per cent of the matings over the course of ten years. So it pays to be a senior male manakin in a top performing team because such a bird is likely to be chosen by as many as fifty or sixty hens a year. However, the cost of that achievement is considerable. It has been estimated that during his apprenticeship as a junior partner, a male will utter about 3 million 'to-le-do' calls and spend about 1000 hours perfecting his cartwheel routine before standing a chance of graduating to the status of a senior male. Then life becomes even more tiring, because he now has to expend extra energy calling for his team mate and performing solo in front of the hen before copulating with her. As a result, a ten-year-old senior male is up to 25 per cent underweight and on the very razor's edge of survival. Nevertheless, as male manakins improve with practice both their singing and dancing, and the hens fall for only the best performers, it follows that only the longest living and thus the best quality males ever get to breed.

But how do the hens discriminate between such a large number of performing males? Apparently, manakins have a very well-developed part of the brain – the hippocampus – which is concerned with memory. This talent is vital for a species which has to remember a large number of sites in the forest where they can obtain ripe fruit. It also enables the hens to recall the difference between a lot of cock birds doing their best to impress!

Leks – the ultimate mate markets

'Lek' is a Swedish term for play, given to a kind of territory held by the males of certain animals – like the manakins – and used solely for sex. Often located in vast, featureless landscapes, these communal meeting places are, for males, the most competitive mate markets on earth. Visits by females characteristically produce a frenzy of courtship as males desperately attempt to outshine each other. Despite showing and sounding off for all they are worth, many of the males will sell nothing because the females are the most critical of shoppers. Each visits the display ground for only a brief period, comparing and contrasting the individual performances of the males in the minutest of detail before making her choice. For males, whether fly, fish or fowl, there is no equality of opportunity. Those that hold the centre ground are overwhelmingly more attractive to the females than others – indeed, the majority of males on a lek fail to make any sexual connection at all.

Leks – or arena displays as they are sometimes called – are highly specialized, and relatively few kinds of animals have evolved them. One feature common to all is that the males play no part in rearing the young, spending part or much of the day

on the lek for weeks or even months on end. How such a mating system originated is a matter for speculation. It is possible that leks began in species which inhabited open landscapes where the sexes had difficulty simply meeting up. In these circumstances, males might have staked out and defended places which females had to visit either to feed or to nest. Such 'hot spots' would certainly have been a magnet to sexually active males and they would have assembled and competed for the best positions to intercept the females. In some cichlids, the males establish their communal display grounds over beds of sand which the females need for depositing their eggs. Nowadays, most arenas have no resources, other than the males and the service they provide for the discerning females.

Great mounds look alike. It takes the eye of an expert female cichlid to see which one is the best of all. She will choose the builder to father her offspring.

There are risks to taking part in these ostentatious mate markets. Mediterranean fruit-flies (Medflies) – *Ceratitis capitata* – are serious pests in citrus orchards because the grubs tunnel into the fruit and destroy their commercial value. As female Medflies have to visit fruiting orange and lemon trees to lay their eggs, this is where the red-eyed males gather in leks to intercept them. Acting alone, they stand only a small chance of mating, but their success at attracting females is greatly improved if they advertise in groups. Up to eight flies gather on adjacent leaves of a citrus tree where they jockey for as central a position as possible. Virgin females are attracted to these fleshpots of sex by the power of the male's alluring perfume. When assessing a male, the female Medfly confronts him on his leaf, whereupon he becomes very excited, frantically buzzing his prettily patterned wings to waft a stream of scent in her direction from a bead of fluid protruding from his anal glands. Should she become enraptured, the couple either consummate their brief courtship on the spot or move off to a more secluded part of the tree. Afterwards, the male returns to his pad while the female heads for the immature fruit where she lays her eggs.

Unfortunately for these insects, participating in high-profile sexual signalling can end in tragedy. Yellow and black common wasps have learned to track the male's seductive scent, with deadly consequences. These wasps, which are widespread in Europe, are voracious hunters, endlessly patrolling the canopies and capturing and macerating their victims with their powerful mandibles. By following the male Medflies' odour plumes back to their source, they have discovered that the leks are a very convenient supply of easy food. Although displaying males are quite alert and can make themselves scarce at the sudden appearance of a foraging wasp, the courting couples are always somewhat preoccupied, especially during the 'buzzing' phase when the female is assessing the displaying male. Most vulnerable of all are copulating couples. They are locked together for up to two hours and, as their bodies are impregnated with sexual odour, the wasps easily smell them out. And of course, the wasp is doubly rewarded for its effort by killing a pair of flies.

This severe predation pressure may be responsible for male Medflies fighting for central positions in the lek, because wasps are more likely to snatch flies from the peripheral positions. Also, flies *in flagrante delicto* tend to leave the lek, although they are not completely safe even after they have retreated behind twigs and foliage – the wasps can still scent them out.

The Medfly's problem is common to most lek species, except that the predators are different. As we shall see, cock sage grouse on the fringes of the lek are taken by golden eagles – and male African topi antelope are vulnerable to hungry hyenas and lions.

Leks are found in many kinds of fish, especially those which occur where the bottom is fairly featureless. Many cichlids which dwell in Lake Malawi breed communally. In places, the sandy lake bed lining the shore resembles a moonscape with the surface raised into a series of mounds and pock-marked in between with numerous craters. These 'bowers', as they are called, represent stalls in the extensive mate markets, created with much labour by various kinds of cichlids. For example, in *Lethrinops*, the blue-banded males defend a breeding area aggressively against all comers, with the exception of the females of their species. The male builds a 'sand castle' which is the centre-piece of his patch of lake bed; shovelling sand into his mouth and releasing it through his gills, he painstakingly constructs a mound about 50 centimetres (20 inches) across and excavates a crater in the top of it. Once finished, the male carefully maintains the structure – if he did not, water currents and wave action would quickly demolish it. Each dished mound is separated from the neighbouring male's by about 3 metres (10 feet), and in one lek there may be between twenty and fifty, each occupied by a lusty fish.

The walled arena is the male's private pad where he seduces any female which ventures over the rim. These aggregations, often in the same place year after year, may greatly assist the sexes to locate each other in an otherwise rather featureless expanse of undulating sand. Once they find the lek, the females are not short of choice as the males work tirelessly to tempt them into their arenas. The mating process follows a fairly consistent routine. As soon as a gravid female approaches a male's territory, he darts out, presents himself broadside to her, erects his fins and quivers his tail to display their full coloration. He then implores her to follow by swimming back to his arena. If she is reluctant, he repeats the process. If the male fails to excite her, the female swims on to find a better one. Eventually, she discovers one which impresses her and follows him into the centre of the arena where she spawns (see Chapter 4 for the fascinating details).

Passing the buck

Among mammals, arena displays are confined almost entirely to a few deer and antelope. In general, the hugely competitive stags and bucks are assiduous mate guarders – during the rut, a dominant red deer stag, which is not a lekking species, will stick to 'his' group of hinds through thick and thin. However, in some species, the females need such a large area over which to forage that the males cannot possible defend them. Under these circumstances, the females roam while the males collect at a communal lek. The classic example is that of the Ugandan kob, an elegant orange-brown antelope whose males sport a handsome pair of lyre-shaped horns.

Kobs live in equatorial Africa where, although the balmy climate enables them to breed all year round, there are twice yearly peaks of sexual activity immediately after the rains. For much of the time, the sexes lead separate lives, the females and their immature offspring coalescing into small herds which range widely across lowland pastures, often close to water, until they individually come into oestrus. To find a worthy mate, they visit one of the traditional mating grounds or arenas where the bucks disport themselves to offer their sexual services. The females may have as many as forty mature males to choose from on a large site, although most of them are smaller and occupied by about a dozen. The male market is nicely laid out because each animal occupies a patch of ground about the size of a putting green, but they are not all equally appealing. The graceful, long-legged females are attracted to the buck with the best address.

Picking their way through the peripheral territories where they hardly give a glance to the owners, nearly all the nervous females end up loitering in the central position held by the dominant male, where the grass is generally greener and located in the open, well away from potentially dangerous cover. The proprietor is invariably a vigorous, muscular male whose status and quality are reflected in the prime position on which he parades.

As it is the most desirable location in the arena, he has had to fight for it and is frequently tested and challenged while holding it. Whistling strenuously, he maintains a defiant pose. With head and tail raised and penis unsheathed, the top male is continuously forced to display his aggressive sexuality and deter lesser bucks. Occasionally he faces more determined challengers, forcing him to engage them with locked horns as each animal attempts to throw the other off balance. Such scraps sometimes end up with one or other of the contestants becoming injured, as the number of bucks in the population with broken horns testifies. At the worst, the loser may die of its injuries.

Precisely what attracts the majority of the 'shoppers' to the dominant buck's address is not altogether clear. They may swoon less at the sight of his good body than at the noticeably strong smell of the ground on which he struts. This is due to the amount of urine sprinkled on the turf by the large number of previously visiting females, indicating that it is a popular and therefore a safe place for them to linger.

The dominant buck rarely needs to hassle his customers. Having made their choice, the females are available to the owner, which courts each of them in turn. He solicits sex with head held low, sniffing the female's rear and causing her to urinate, perhaps catching some drops on his muzzle. For most mammals with a much more refined sense of smell than we have, the liquid is not just a waste product to be excreted and forgotten, but a medium for passing messages. So it is with the Ugandan kob; the hormones and perhaps other odoriferous chemicals it contains accurately chart the female's progress towards her brief period of sexual receptivity. The male monitors this by regularly sampling her urine, the taste and scent of which he savours by wrinkling his nose and curling his upper lip back. If it smells right, the buck becomes excited, moving in such a way as to draw attention to the black stripes on his legs and lifting his chin to show off the white chevron on his throat. If the female is ready, she allows him to approach from behind and touch her body with a stiffly raised foreleg, whereupon he mounts her and inseminates her with a single, rapid thrust.

Fending off challenge after challenge and servicing a succession of females inevitably saps the central buck of energy. Distracted from feeding, he loses condition and becomes exhausted; after two or three days he is usually toppled from his eagerly sought position by a fresher and more robust rival. After perhaps a fight and a lengthy chase, the vanquished male either retires to a less demanding position at the periphery of the arena or withdraws altogether to lick his wounds and begin to restore his strength for another mating period.

OVERLEAF A red light district for Ugandan kob. The males advertise their services and the females come shopping for sex. Males defending the best patches of savannah get more customers.

Sex in the sage brush

The sage-brush country of the American 'Wild West' is not perhaps the most inspiring landscape that the great subcontinent can offer. Much of its scenery consists of endless rolling plains covered by a uniform grey-green carpet of vegetation, relieved only by occasional alkaline basins, rocky buttes and ranges of hills which, in places, rise into ranges such as the Sierra Nevadas. And yet this tedious sage-brush 'tundra' is the setting for one of the most colourful mate markets in the USA. From the end of February to the middle of May, cock sage grouse – the largest and most spectacular of the North American grouse – gather to sell themselves as the best of their sex. The hens are the 'buyers'; they alone will decide which ones come up to scratch.

Sage grouse are very much birds of the brush; lacking a gizzard, their digestive systems can cope only with the tender young shoots of sage, and their plumage is superbly camouflaged, rendering both sexes all but invisible in the scrubby vegetation during much of the year. However, as the mating season approaches, sage grouse start to become conspicuous, congregating daily on their traditional strutting grounds to court and copulate. The birds arrive well before sunrise in the sheltered basins where the displays are generally held. Although as many as 200 or more males used to assemble in such places, nowadays, with falling numbers, about fifty is a good gathering. Each strutting ground is spread over an area about the size of a football pitch and each cock has his own small parade ground centred perhaps on a slight elevation which he defends from rival males. As they take up their positions, they spread their tails, puff up their chests and start to stomp.

Sage grouse are extraordinarily handsome birds – indeed, their displays were the inspiration for the ceremonial costumes and dances performed by native people of the Sioux tribe who shared the plains with them. At the prospect of sex, a male grouse erects his tail into an eye-catching fan of twenty spiky feathers which, when seen from the front, frames the breast, where his most remarkable adornments are located. On either side of his chest, he sports a pair of orange-skinned air sacs; these are set in a fulsome stole of glistening white feathers which hangs virtually to the ground. When inflated, the sacs resemble two poached eggs 'sunny-side up' and add considerable impact to the cock's strutting display.

After taking a few mincing steps forward with his wings held stiffly against his flanks, the bird draws back his head and jerks the air sacs several times until they deflate with a loud plop that is audible several hundred metres away. This is accompanied by a swishing noise made by the bristly breast feathers rubbing against the drooping wings. After each bout, the cock remains motionless for a few seconds and then repeats the routine, directing it either at neighbouring males or at any hens which might be around.

While the cock birds work themselves up into a dancing frenzy, the hens play it cool. Between fifty and seventy may turn up at a large arena, nonchalantly walking around, occasionally pecking at the ground and seemingly unimpressed by the antics of the cocks. However, despite their apparent apathy, the hens are present for one reason only – to be inseminated before disappearing into the sage bushes to rear their families as single mothers. In fact, the evidence shows that they are taking everything in, carefully weighing the cocks up against each other – perhaps assessing the vigour of their stomping, the splendour of their plumage and the position of their individual strutting territories within the arena. Having made her choice, a hen solicits by simply squatting down in front of the cock, and he mounts her – sometimes awkwardly, as he is half as heavy again as she is – and mates.

In the end, the modestly attired females tend to be unanimous in their choice, loitering in tight groups close to where the largest and most dominant male performs for all he is worth. No one is quite sure what the hens find so attractive about the 'master cock', as he is called. He is generally a fit and energetic specimen, top of the pecking order, and has probably fought for and won control over the highest mound in the arena, from which he lords it over his lesser neighbours. As older and thus more experienced birds tend to shift towards the central positions, perhaps age rather than beauty is the key to attaining the mating 'hot spot'. Whatever it is that gives the male sex appeal, the hens overwhelmingly choose the same bird to father their next brood. In one arena, for instance, the master cock performed three quarters of the 174 matings. In another, 90 per cent of the hens were mated by only 10 per cent of the males.

But there is a price to pay for standing out in the crowd. What catches the attention of the hens is just as likely to be seen by predators. Dominant stud sage grouse are at serious risk from discerning hunters like golden eagles. Soaring well above the sage brush, the sharp-eyed eagles lock on to the robust and colourful birds at the centre of the arenas. The master cocks often fail to see the deadly predator swooping down on them, perhaps because they are preoccupied by the presence of competing males and solicitous hens. However, by the time they are killed, they have won the sexual lottery, having been chosen to fertilize the majority of the local hens and thus having succeeded in spreading their superior genes.

LEFT Strutting his stuff. A hen's-eye view of a male sage grouse showing off. The full display of these arena birds inspired the ritual dances of the native American Sioux people.

RIGHT A dazzling dandy. A male king bird of paradise is a glorious tribute to the creative power of female choice.

The most beautiful mates of all

Various other kinds of grouse, and the related pheasants and peacocks, are members of the select club of arena birds. Sex on leks is also practised in a few exotic wildfowl, some humming-birds, most manakins, cocks of the rock, whydahs and several weaver-birds. Perhaps the most surprising species to engage in communal courtship are the ruff and the great snipe – both waders which nest on the wide open tundra – and the kakapo, a virtually flightless parrot from New Zealand currently teetering on the brink of extinction. However, the most resplendent of all lek breeders are to be found among the forty-two kinds of birds of paradise.

If just one group of creatures is to be taken to illustrate the sheer creative force of female choice, then the birds of paradise have to be it. Their very name reflects our sense of abject wonder at their surreal splendour and the exuberant beauty of the males. Even the place where all but four live, in the rain-forests of New Guinea and neighbouring small islands, adds to their mystique. This superficially diverse family, embracing the sicklebills, parotias, long-tailed astrapias, blue-black manucodes and the heavily plumed paradiseas, has evolved from crow-like birds. Their exotic nature is due to a quirk of geography; the deep-water channel which acts as a barrier separating the islands of South-East Asia from Australasia has kept out the arboreal squirrels and macaques, thus leaving the forests clear of competition for these fruit-eating birds.

No description does justice to the ornate appearance of the birds of paradise. Most have long lacy feathers extending well beyond the tail, but during courtship these are erected over the back in swirling sprays of vividly coloured plumes which are shaken as the birds bow and dance in excitement. Wings are rhythmically flapped and in some species such as Wallace's standard wing the breast shield is expanded and pulsed to show off the jewel-like iridescence of the feathers, especially if caught in a beam of early morning sunlight. The males, throbbing with sexual expectation, accompany their stunning performances with raucous calls or mechanical buzzing noises.

The Raggiana bird of paradise, a fairly common species of the eastern and southern regions of Papua New Guinea, is one of the most familiar as it adorns the official crest of that country and is the emblem advertising both its official airline and the most widely consumed brand of lager. Commercial considerations aside, a cock Raggiana in his prime is among the most ostentatious 'living billboards' of the family. He has a golden yellow head with matching 'epaulettes' on his wings, an oily green throat and a deep maroon chest, both with the appearance of plush velvet. From the centre of his tail emerge a pair of wire-like feathers extending an arm's length beyond the tip, but most magnificent of all are the tufts of apricot-coloured plumes which project from the flanks for up to 50 centimetres (20 inches). At their extremities, they are lace-like and when fluffed up and shimmering in a shaft of light they are both conspicuous and breathtakingly beautiful. As if this is not enough, the birds have piercing yellow eyes and powder-blue beaks.

Groups of cocks perform their communal displays high up in the canopy at traditional sites around the forests. They assemble in their respective leks just before dawn when the mist still lies in the valleys, and begin by creating a surprising racket, with their shrill nasal calls acting as sound beacons for the hens. As the sun breaks the horizon and catches the top of the ridges where many of the arboreal courts are situated, parties of dowdy females flit over the canopy, visiting one group of males after another. As the males in a court catch sight of them, they strike up their strident chorus and break into a flurry of frenzied display, each male on his own perch, bowing, waving his wings and showing off his cascade of orange plumes. As in all arena displays, one of the males occupies a central position which is clearly more attractive to the hens, while the others form a backing to his passionate performance. Should any of the hens land, all of the males in the lek may freeze in full display.

The females appear unimpressed by the bizarre but spectacular antics being acted out before them. Despite the energy of the cocks' performances, the hens usually depart. Sometimes, one of them may take a special interest in the 'master cock', inspecting his vent closely when he bows deeply to erect the plumes over his back. Nevertheless, she is usually dismissive and flies off to another court. This is female choice in action. No hasty decisions here! However, on about one in 10 visits, a hen might fall for the leading male and solicit sex from him. Standing beside her, he pummels her back with his wings for perhaps half a minute. If she is still convinced that he is a top-quality cock, she allows him to mount, their cloacas 'kiss' while he transfers sperm and then she retires to raise their joint offspring by herself. An hour after sunrise, all activity in the Raggiana's leks is over until perhaps late in the afternoon, when there is a minor resurgence of displaying.

But why should sexual dimorphism be extreme in some species and virtually absent in others? This may be influenced by the nature of the bird's food and foraging 'behaviour'. For example, the trumpet manucode feeds on figs. Although these are nutritious, the efforts of both sexes are necessary to collect the amount of food required by the youngsters. In these birds, the sexes are monogamous and look very similar. On the other hand, Raggiana's birds of paradise and many other strongly sexually dimorphic species feed on complex rain-forest fruits such as those of the mahogany or nutmeg tree. They are large and packed with nutrients and the hens alone are able to collect enough of them to support the nestlings. This leaves the males free to pursue a life of relative leisure and sex. They are able to intercept more females in their arboreal courts and advertise for mates with their showy plumage and far-carrying calls. The downside for the males is that relatively few of them ever get to copulate because of the fierce competition in the courts.

Such gaudy, glittering males are the ultimate products of the female's discerning eye – noisy fops of little use except as providers of sperm. By continually choosing the most colourful sexual partners, the fastidious females have moulded and fashioned their mates into these gorgeous receptacles for testes.

But even in making this union, the sexes are often at odds with each other and take quite remarkable steps to ensure that their partners do not cheat. Competition between males also continues with the sexual connection.

3

THE SEXUAL CONNECTION

S ex is personified by the meeting and fusion of male and female gametes – the sperms and eggs which carry the genetic instructions to create a new individual. For fully terrestrial creatures, reaching this stage is a great challenge, because fertilization has to occur inside the female's body – otherwise the eggs and sperms would dry out and die. In the act of coupling, we might be forgiven for believing that the participating individuals were at last in agreement, behaving as a team with the common objective of making new life.

But the apparent harmony is an illusion, because the transfer of semen is by no means a guarantee of conception. In creatures which form partnerships, the female may have had to make do with a less than desirable mate for support, and then rely upon surreptitious affairs to obtain better genes for her off-spring. In turn, the males may have their sights set on other partners. So, even in the final and most crucial stages of procreation, there is still time for both participants to deceive each other and perhaps better their genetic investment. The internal route through the female's body to her eggs is relatively long and exhausting for the minuscule sperms, and she may be able to assist or impede their progress according to circumstances. Furthermore, aping the brawling males who produced them, sperm from different males still find opportunities for competition in the sweep-stake – the race for the eggs. In this crucial tournament, there are no prizes for second place; out of the millions of lashing sperm, just a few winners will take all.

PREVIOUS PAGES
Bull's-eye: a triumphant bull elephant appears to have won the first round in the battle to mate. But will he be the father of her calf?

This chapter is about some of the obvious and some of the surprising ways in which females force sperms to prove their worth before reaching their goal, and how males bypass – or cheat their way past – any obstacles put in the way of their gametes. The quest for conception – which is fundamentally what the battle of the sexes is all about – has driven the evolution of bodily design, the greatest natural technology race on earth. As both sexes 'strive' to take control of the process of fertilization, the females develop hurdles for sperm to overcome, and the sperm's delivery systems – the males – counter with cunning copulatory devices and practices which raise the odds on ensuring their success.

This aspect of sexual strife is universal, even among lowly creatures such as millipedes, whose intricate love life belies their simple nature.

There is often more to intercourse than meets the eye! Typically shy of light, millipedes inhabit crevices, emerging chiefly at night to worm their way through leaf mould and damp soil to munch plant material. During the breeding season, the males become hyperactive and scurry around looking for mates. In these highly promiscuous species, every male is under pressure to intercept as many females as possible before they have been inseminated. When successful, the male takes the active role in initiating a sexual embrace. Running up the back of his partner, he grips her with the pads on his numerous legs and then entwines his body so that both partners come to rest head to head, with their ventral surfaces opposed. In one species, *Julus scandinavius*, the male presents the female with an edible secretion from glands on his second pair of legs, which keeps her occupied while he busies himself transferring his sperm into her.

The arrangement of bodies is crucial, because coupling millipedes must line up their respective paired genitalia before they can consummate their act. Hers open just behind her head, on the second segment, while his are a little further back, on his seventh. When the couple is properly aligned, the male inflates his mating organs and works them into the female's open receptacles. Here they remain for up to two hours, during which time the male passes a package of sperm into receptacles within her body (spermathecae). Here, the sperms are stored until the female needs them.

The shape of the male's intromittent organs – those he uses to insert sperm into the female's body – almost defies description. Normally withdrawn into the body, they are no ordinary tubes for piping the gametes into the female. Fashioned from a pair of legs, the gonopods (as they are called) are so unbelievably complex that they clearly fulfil some other agenda. Consisting of three parts, the organ is equipped with a flagellum and mobile 'wings'. During copulation, the base (called a telopodite) is rhythmically retracted and released, causing the rest of the organ to twist and turn like a trowel inside the female's vulva. What the male is doing is waging war on alien sperm!

Sperm wars

The millipede's priapic complexity goes to the very heart of the battle of the sexes. Males throughout the whole of the animal kingdom can never guarantee the outcome of making the sexual connection; they are eternally at risk either of being cuckolded or of wasting sperm on females who have already been inseminated. In millipedes and many other terrestrial invertebrates, the male's problem is compounded by the female's capacity to store sperm from several partners. Although highly advantageous to females, this state of affairs is not in the male's interest, because it extends the period of intense rivalry beyond courtship and copulation, with sperm from different males racing each other to the eggs. Females have a vested interest in encouraging the reproductive sweepstakes inside them on the grounds that the fastest gametes may come from the most vigorous and 'fittest' males.

In evolutionary terms, the lack of parental certainty has presented males with a challenge, because much of what they get up to when mating seems designed to scupper the chances of rival sperm reaching the eggs. This is especially true for animals in whom the last male to mate tends to father most of the brood. In these highly competitive circumstances, any male which can first rid the female's storage sacs of sperm from previous matings and prevent his own subsequently being usurped puts his own at a tremendous advantage. This seems to be the purpose of the millipede's writhing 'penises'; the scooping movements they perform during copulation displace the semen stockpiled in the female's sperm sacs from previous trysts before the incumbent male deposits his own. Sperm wars are a phenomenon which has shaped the nature of terrestrial sex and have resulted in a veritable Kama Sutra of weird and wonderful mating tools and techniques.

More than meets the eye. The sexual embrace of giant millipedes conceals the male's amazingly complex penis at work removing semen from the female's previous encounters before introducing his own.

A sexual revolution was essential before animals could become fully emancipated from water. Although many of the first primitive land animals evolved a waterproof 'skin', their gametes remained highly vulnerable to desiccation. The first step to achieving internal fertilization was for the females to closet their eggs within the comfortable environs of their own bodies. Sperms had to be vigorous enough to survive being jettisoned in their own aqueous medium into a hostile world. The first true land lovers probably packaged droplets of semen in sealed capsules – spermatophores – to prevent the air from shrivelling up the delicate sperms. These were then taken up by the females during courtship, much as velvet mites and scorpions do today. Although some of the latter creatures live in moist, humid places, the fact that many manage to thrive in the hottest and driest of deserts testifies to the effectiveness of the protection. These venomous little animals perfected their sex act over 100 million years before our reptilian ancestors were displaying the precursor of the penis.

ABOVE Packaged sex: a male katydid passes his sperms to a female wrapped in a protective packet – a spermatophore. The female will eat the part projecting from her abdomen.

LEFT Swollen with desire: the palp of a male nursery-web spider is full of semen and poised for insertion into the large female's genital tract.

But there is an even older technique practised by the velvet worm *Peripatus*, a strange-looking creature that lives in the damp forests of New Zealand. About 8 centimetres (3 inches) long, the velvet worm sports about twenty pairs of short, baggy legs. It is a relict from the age, perhaps 500 million years ago, when the land was being colonized. The velvet worm's sex act is appropriately rudimentary. When ready to breed, the male goes for a stroll and simply places a capsule containing highly tenacious sperms at random on a female's body. Where he sticks his precious gift is immaterial, because tissue-engulfing white blood cells in the female's body migrate to the spot beneath the spermatophore and excavate a passage through which the sperms wriggle into the bloodstream. Once there in force, they make their way to the eggs and fertilize them.

From such beginnings have blossomed a whole spectrum of sex acts, especially among the invertebrates, many of which involve the use of unusual mechanical structures for fighting the sperm wars. Male spiders possess unique 'tools' for the job and have a three-stage technique of inseminating a female. On either side of the jaws, they brandish a pair of hollow palps, the tips of which are greatly swollen and function like fountain-pen fillers. Before the male goes courting, he fills each of them with semen. Firstly he spins a small silken hammock, the purpose of which is to catch drops of semen as they exude from the sexual pores beneath his abdomen. When there is sufficient, he dips the open ends of his copulatory organs into the pool of ejaculated fluid and, by the sucking action of the built-in bulbs, fills the receptacles with it. Sperm induction – as this process is called – may be a long-drawn-out business, taking up to four hours in the case of the large bird-eating spiders. With the palps fully charged, the male is ready to impregnate a mate with them.

Spider-like relatives of the true spiders use different parts of their anatomy. Rare tropical ricinulids possess copulatory organs situated at the tips of their third pair of legs. Solifuges – or sun spiders – use their jaws. These aggressive, carnivorous hunters scuttle around the arid and semi-desert regions of the world, looking like large, hairy spiders and moving so fast that in South Africa they are referred to as 'Kalahari Ferraris'. One species, called *Solpuga*, is the sabre-toothed tiger of the invertebrate world, with a 'stone-age' courtship to match. The males leap on to prospective mates, which play possum while being dragged off to be impregnated. Once a male has a female in his clutches, he sets about her with his hunting sabres, massaging and widening her sexual opening. After releasing a drop of semen on to his fangs, he uses them vigorously to rub the suspension of sperms into her. When finished, he pinches the edges of her orifice together, leaving his gametes to race for her eggs.

No other group of animals rivals the insects in the intricate designs of their genitalia. This is not altogether surprising. Being such prolific breeders and with a rapid turnover of generations, insects have the capacity to evolve in the fast lane. In the all-pervading struggle to breed, the sexes are locked into their own contest; any male which displays an innovation that guarantees paternity will be at an advantage, but females 'retaliate' with counter-measures to encourage rivalry between potential partners so that only the most worthy will father their offspring. It is rather like an escalating arms race except that, in this case, it is not weapons to kill but accessory organs to make new life that are subject to continuous change under the pressure of natural selection. In insects, this has been a fantastically innovative force, and the variety of their copulatory organs and their innovative sexual behaviour are expressions of it.

The fly's twisted tale

Sometimes they are baffling. Miriam Rothschild, a British naturalist and the world's leading expert on fleas, once remarked despairingly that the male parasite's relatively huge sexual apparatus – with its double-barrelled mating rods which uncoil like a spring inside the female – was so complicated that it did not make sense! In most other insects, the mechanics are easier to understand. The external genitalia are situated at the tip of the abdomen. Consisting in the males of claspers, various plates and a 'penis', the anatomy often ensures that copulation is possible only when both male and female are precisely aligned like a lock and key. The structure of the male's rear end certainly prevents breeding between different species.

The female's anatomy is also complex. The sperm-storage organs range from relatively simple sacs to highly convoluted organs at the end of tortuous tubes, the latter perhaps limiting the male's access and giving the female a measure of control over the outcome of copulation. Such layouts give the impression that the females are testing the ingenuity of the males by confronting their sperms with an ever more challenging course to their eggs. The males counter the handicap with ever longer and more complex intromittent organs to give their own sperms a head start. Such is the severity of the tussle between the sexes that the male Mediterranean fruit-fly has been driven to develop a monstrous 'penis'. It is equivalent to 40 per cent of his body length and terminates in a snake-like structure. During copulation, the male unwinds his penis and threads it through the female's long ovipositor (the external organ through which she lays her eggs). Then, with various lobes expanding and contracting, the tip is inched along her winding internal tract until it eventually reaches the chamber which receives the seminal fluid.

ABOVE The puzzling penis. The rear anatomy of a male flea is of baffling complexity, and is the outcome of a sexual arms' race.

OPPOSITE Sperm wars. A male damsel fly (the upper one) removes all rival sperm from inside the female with his bizarre, customized penis situated just behind his legs.

Mating even involves a serious twist in the tail for some male flies. Again, this may be a testament to the creative power unleashed by the war of the sperm. Flies copulate in the 'inverse interlock' position, in which the top of the male's sexual paraphernalia clasps the bottom of the female's anatomy. In some species, such as the house-fly, this involves the abdomen in a 360-degree twist about its axis during development. With the assistance of a cat's cradle of muscles, the torsion causes the gut and reproductive organs to loop around each other and the fly's external body segments become deformed in the process. The mating technique that requires such a fundamental alteration of the male's genital geography probably traces its origins to the first flies. These might have mated on the wing, as mayflies do today, with the males engaging the females' rear ends from underneath. True flies now mate on solid surfaces with the male uppermost and guarding his prize, but the genitalia retain their original connections, turning him into a sexual contortionist.

The drive to help sperm on their journey and to bypass any other obstacles set by females has resulted in another bizarre form of 'copulation' – often performed in beds! Bedbugs once inhabited bat caves and the dens of large European mammals. Now they are better known as denizens of dirty doss houses and squalid accommodation, and emerge at night to crawl stealthily between the bedclothes to suck blood, leaving only an irritating blotch on the skin as a memento of their visit.

The males avoid the normal genital route of inseminating their mates in favour of a rapid but uniquely barbarous method. They drive their penis like a hypodermic syringe through the body wall of the female and inject sperm directly into the cavity occupied by circulating blood (the haemocoel). The process is known, appropriately, as 'traumatic insemination'! Some of the sperm are destroyed by the female's immune system, but the tough ones travel to the ovaries and accumulate in a special storage gland where they lodge until needed. The female produces a batch of eggs after she has taken a meal of blood, and some sperm are let out to fertilize them. Despite the apparent trauma, the female bedbugs have adjusted to this form of sex by evolving a special abdominal tissue (known as the organ of Berlese) that assists in the healing of the wound left by the male.

When the females are endowed with perfectly normal mating organs, why have the males adopted such a violent-looking insemination technique? Certainly by injecting his sperm directly into his mate's body, a male may gain an advantage over slower and more orthodox competitors, and also avoid being blocked by vaginal plugs or any of the various forms of chastity belts and scoops that abound in the insect world (see later). Once swimming safely in the female's blood, the sperm are unstoppable.

Some of the best studies on how males cope with sperm competition have been made on damsel and dragonflies, and support the theory that intromittent organs play an important role in the male's struggle to ensure his paternity.

Sex among damsels and dragons

The unique choreography of sex in damsel and dragonflies is as elegant as it is complex. The 5500 species belong to an ancient group of insects that can be traced back 300 million years ago to the time when our coal seams were being laid down. Then as now, they spent much of their lives as aquatic larvae, emerging as acrobatic flyers utterly dependent upon sharp vision for intercepting other insects. As befits such graceful aeronauts, over three quarters of their bulk is accounted for by their wing muscles – the engines for their four broad wings – which, weight for weight, deliver more power than any other muscle in the animal kingdom. In order to copulate successfully, both sexes need very flexible bodies.

Male damsels, for instance, hold territories which include open water where the females can deposit their eggs without getting snagged by pond weed. They are very active, using stored body fat to give them sufficient stamina to patrol and defend their patch for perhaps ten days; this gives them plenty of opportunities to mate. Like other insects, the males produce sperm from the terminal segments of their long, narrow bodies, but the damsel's curious coupling technique has developed because the sperm has to be consigned to a storage chamber on the underside of the abdomen just behind the thorax. The transfer is made by looping the abdomen to bring the tip to meet the openings of the chamber. When a likely female arrives in a male's part of the pond or river, his first act is to seize her thorax with a pair of claspers on the end of his 'tail' so that the couple move in tandem, with the male leading.

The act of copulation commences when the pair adopts the 'wheel' position; the female flexes her body so that the vagina at the tip of her abdomen docks with the male's accessory penis, which links to his sperm-storage sac. His organ is an amazing structure, shaped to fit the female's reproductive canal, but topped by a flagellum which is articulated and shaped like a scoop. This is what goes to work before any sperm is transferred; the male starts a rhythmic pumping action as the flagellum reaches into the innermost recesses of the female's storage area and clears out any sperm from previous matings. In some damselflies, this behaviour accounts for 90 per cent of the duration of the sex act, which may be as long as a couple of hours. Only when the male has thoroughly scraped out his partner's sperm chamber will he ejaculate.

Dragonflies have a similar sex life, although some of the details differ. For example, the male black-tailed skimmer (*Orthretum cancellatum*) has a flagellum shaped like a pipe-cleaner with backward-projecting spines that rid the female of any lingering sperm. This takes some time to erect and work its way to the storage chamber. Accordingly, the males enforce a relatively long period of copulation – approximately fifteen minutes. On the other hand, in the four-spotted chaser dragonfly (*Libellulia quadrimaculatus*), a flat-bodied species, copulation on the wing is brief because the penis is furnished with a tip like a beach-ball which inflates quickly as the male's blood pressure rises. The penis enters the sperm-storage organ and packs the rival semen against the wall, making a space for the male's contribution next to the entrance, where it will be strategically placed to be first out to fertilize the eggs – provided the female does not copulate again!

Land vertebrates are not quite so enterprising as insects in the way they make the sexual connection. Their generations have a much slower

Penis power

turnover, and the relatively smaller populations mean that the engine of evolution works more slowly because innovations are thrown up less often. And yet the same considerations prevail. In the paranoid quest for as many partners as possible, males attempt to scatter their seed in all directions, and females, in the search for the perfect male, ideally like to keep their options open by encouraging rivalry between sperm from different mates. Whether aphid or elephant, ensuring paternity is an issue that exercises males, and females still seek the best fathers for their offspring. However, there is an important difference between insects and the higher vertebrates, as females on the whole do not store sperm, so those injected by the first male to copulate during a female's fertile period have a commanding advantage in the race for the eggs. Whereas insects and their kin have invested heavily in genital paraphernalia to slug out the sperm wars, the vertebrates are driven much more by brain power and behaviour in settling matters of paternity. Outright aggression between males over access to females is therefore prevalent among terrestrial vertebrates, and coy females more often exercise their choice of mating partner after making males woo them with prolonged and elaborate courtship.

The penis is crucial for the intimate style of vertebrate sex. Fitting snugly into the vaginal barrel, it binds mates together during intercourse. The organ undoubtedly helped different lines of amphibious vertebrates to defeat the problems of breeding high and dry. Long ago, our reptilian ancestors evolved the hard-shelled egg which encapsulated the embryo in its own private puddle until it was old enough to hatch. However, the development of the eggs had to start before each became sealed and wrapped, requiring the sperms to intercept the naked ova high up in the female's reproductive tract. In a sense, the penis might have been a solution to the problem – a nozzle which could pipe semen into the female and achieve internal fertilization. Such devices enabled reptiles, among the vertebrates, as well as a whole range of animals without backbones, to become land lovers.

Penises come in all shapes and sizes. Among the higher vertebrates, lizards and snakes have a double copulatory organ. The advantage of this arrangement seems to be that, as both sexes have tails which tend to get in the way of any form of cloacal intimacy, insertion by the male is most easily achieved by a tube projecting sideways while he coils around the female's hips. By possessing a pair of shafts – called hemipenes – the male is equally prepared for a left- or right-flank sexual engagement. The shafts usually lie inside out when not in use, but during copulation they are everted by rising blood pressure and muscular contraction. Each is connected to a testis and is furnished with spines and hooks which anchor it firmly inside the female's body.

Inseparable couple. The backward-facing spines on the male tiger's penis makes it impossible for the pair to part until he loses his erection.

Some snakes have truly awesome organs. South African burrowing snakes possess a pair of worm-like rods practically as long as their tail. In venomous vipers, each of their two hemipenes are as deeply forked as a snake's tongue. A male rattlesnake has the equivalent of a pair of double-headed penises, each ideally constructed to anchor inside the female's vent. When turned 'inside out', each resembles a medieval mace, studded with vicious, backward-projecting hooks that inevitably bite into the female's cloacal walls during intercourse. Such cruel decorations undoubtedly prevent the hemipene from being prematurely disengaged before the male has delivered his semen. Furthermore, the uncomfortable lacerations they inflict might deter the female from indulging in further sexual relations that season, so guaranteeing the male his paternity. Tortoises and crocodiles cope adequately with a single central penis, as of course do mammals.

The mammalian penis has a dual function, not only serving to pipe semen into the vagina, but also doubling up as a spout for directing urine away from the body. For most of the time it fulfils the latter role and is folded away, shrunken or sheathed. Only during serious sexual encounters does it spring into action, stiffened in some way and ready to be thrust into the lubricated vulva of a female. Although a simple tube would presumably accomplish the job, there is an extraordinary range of penis shapes and sizes in mammals – all the better to deliver sperm as near as possible to the eggs and to supplant those lingering from previous matings with other males.

Mammalian penises can be divided broadly into two types depending upon how they are readied for intercourse – some are instantly 'available', while others have to wait for the blood pressure to make them rigid.

Echidnas or spiny anteaters are, like duck-billed platypuses, egg-laying mammals and retain several characteristics of their reptilian ancestors, such as a cloaca – the terminal part of the gut into which the kidney and reproductive ducts open. The males sport a baffling intromittent organ pumped up with blood. Usually sheathed until the final stages of foreplay, it is an incredible four-headed structure, and each of its cauliflower-like tips releases semen. The arrangement must help to direct the fluid into every corner of the female's cloaca. Coupling lasts three hours, thus preventing any other males from mounting, after which the partners ripple their prickles and go their separate ways.

The vascular organs of male monkeys, apes, horses, tapirs, elephants, rhinos and whales are all erected by a combination of blood pressure and clever plumbing! The shafts contain columns of spongy tissue attached at one end to the pubic bones and become grossly tumescent when gorged with blood. This happens during sexual arousal when the arteries servicing the erectile tissue are widened and the corresponding veins draining the organ are partly strangled by special muscles. Pumping up the penis with blood takes a little time for larger mammals – a tapir may take two minutes to achieve an erection long enough for the head (or glans) to reach between its front legs – and so species like this, with hydraulically operated organs, often engage in periods of titillation before they mate.

Double-barrelled weapon. Male water snakes have two hemipenes for sexually engaging the female from one side or the other. *Drawing by Birgitte Bruun.*

The tips of penises vary in shape from species to species. Some are flattened like pistons, others have flanged tips. They are certainly not for display. A clue to their function is provided by the fact that the most florid designs tend to be found in species in which the females are likely to mate with more than one partner. This scenario promotes sperm competition, a fact which has led to the suggestion that penises furnished with flanged and ridged heads may be able to ream out semen from previous matings as they are moved in and out of the vagina. Such an interpretation has been used to explain the flanged tip of a man's penis.

Those of the cat family are equipped with backward-projecting spines that impede its withdrawal – at least while the erection is maintained. It is likely that the barbs provide a powerful stimulus to the female's vagina, because the cat is one of a large number of species – including rabbits and North American mole shrews – in which the excitement of mating triggers the release of eggs from the ovaries.

To work effectively, the inflated penis must be maintained in a sufficiently rigid state. Many mammals, among them several kinds of monkeys and rodents, ensure that their penises do not crumple under the pressure of vigorous coupling by the presence of a bone – or baculum – that adds extra stiffness to the shaft. Those of seals, sea-lions and walruses are especially well developed.

The largest penises in the world are vascular ones. The bulls of all five species of rhino have very lengthy ones when sexually excited, and each is capped by a series of curious lobes reminiscent of a purplish daffodil. The problem faced by these and other large mammals is that once the male has mounted his partner, he can no longer see the female's sexual bulls-eye. In rhinos, as the bull's ardour blossoms, the head of his penis starts to weave around until it makes contact with the vulva. Once the tip engages, the remainder of the shaft is 'walked in' and remains there for perhaps half an hour.

Fully grown bull African elephants also have a mechanical difficulty during their rare bouts of pachydermous passion. Weighing up to nearly 10 tonnes, they are rigidly constructed and incapable of gyrating their pelvis to dock their penis. The cows have evolved an unusual genital lay-out to assist intercourse – their vaginal opening has relocated from the usual position beneath the anus to a site under their baggy bellies where you would expect to find a navel. This saves the bull from having to attempt the impossible task of bringing his groin close up against his mate's thighs in order to copulate.

Although the cow elephant's low-slung vulva is much easier to reach, the bull still has to mount her, putting great stress not only on her legs, but also on his own hind quarters. Young cows occasionally break a leg as a result of being chased and mounted by heavyweight males. Once in position, much of the action is performed by the bull's 'motorized' penis. It is a monster, weighing 25 kilograms (55 pounds) and extending nearly 2 metres (6 foot 6 inches) under the influence of a pounding heart. The jumbo penis is also a veritable power-pack, containing not only erectile tissue but its own engine of muscles, enabling it to thrash around, searching for the vaginal opening. Shaped rather like a hook, it is well adapted for reaching a long way beneath the female's belly and probing upwards, penetrating deeply into her low-slung receptacle to make contact with the cervix. After performing a few piston-like thrusts, the bull ejaculates. Once mating is complete, competition from other males forces the bull to protect his paternity by guarding the cow for a while, preventing her from taking another partner whose sperm might usurp his own.

RIGHT Pumped up by passion. Like many mammals, the zebra stallion's penis is inflated by blood pressure. The flattened tip behaves like a piston, ramming the sperms as close to the eggs as possible.

BELOW Muscularly mobile: the crooked penis of an elephant is well adapted for seeking the female's vaginal opening beneath her belly.

Instant erections are possible for males which possess fibro-elastic penises. These are stowed away and ready to use in the bellies of cud-chewing beasts such as deer, antelope, sheep and cattle. Each instrument of sperm transfer is like a poker, formed largely from hard gristle, and does not rely much upon blood pressure to mobilize it. A couple of kinks along the shaft allows it to be folded back under tension into a neat S-shaped arrangement in the male's belly. When the retractor muscle is relaxed, the penis springs out of its sheath and can be stabbed straight into the rear of a receptive female. The bull injects a dose of sperm in an instant, and the retractor muscle withdraws the penis, flexing it back into shape inside the bull's belly for protection. Not all fibro-elastic penises are the same shape. The ram's terminates in a thumb-length filament called a filiform appendage. During intromission, it rotates rapidly like a propeller and sprays semen round the cervix. For members of the pig family, mating has an unusual twist. The boars have long, slim penises with tips uniquely shaped like corkscrews that drill into the sow's vagina during intercourse, releasing well over half a litre (up to 1½ pints) of semen in the process.

One might be forgiven for thinking that the largest testes in the world reside in the bodies of

Gonads great and small

the world's biggest beasts – bull blue whales. But although a fully grown specimen reaches 30 metres (100 feet) in length and weighs 150 tonnes, it has comparatively puny gonads inside its belly. Relative to the size of their bodies, they are about the size and weight of a man's. A much smaller whale boasts the record for the biggest sperm factory in the world. The right whale is about half the bulk of a blue whale and yet its gonads are 3 metres (10 feet) long and weigh half a tonne. The reason for this discrepancy lies in the different mating arrangements of the two species. Right whales are promiscuous: whenever a female comes into breeding condition, she is accompanied by several bulls, all of whom she allows to mate with her. Competition between sperm is therefore intense and, under these circumstances, males with giant gonads which can turn out billions of sperms stand a better chance of competing in the race for paternity. Bull blue whales apparently have no such worries: they face little opposition and are accordingly less well endowed.

BELOW The champions: among mammals, the tiny honey possum (left) has proportionately the largest testes. Among birds, the male superb blue fairy wren (right) has relatively the biggest gonads – 25 per cent of its body weight.

However, one of the smallest of mammals has the largest gonads for its size of any comparable creature. A nectar-feeding marsupial from Western Australia, the diminutive honey possum has testes equivalent

to 4 per cent of its body weight which manufacture super-sperms forty times longer in absolute terms than those of a man or a right whale. Male honey possums are highly sexed and competitive, and the huge testes churn out plenty of 'ammunition' to enhance their chances of achieving paternity.

For any given species, the relative size of the testes says much about the level of sperm competition faced by the males. Among the great apes, silver-backed male gorillas are certainly the heavyweights, but they are so modestly endowed that their scrota are difficult to discern. Tipping the scales at 250 kilograms (550 pounds), a male gorilla is four times the size of a chimpanzee and yet the chimpanzee's testes are six times the weight of a gorilla's. Again, the reason for this apparent paradox lies in their different mating arrangements. Gorillas live in stable families in which a dominant male is master of all he surveys and has unchallenged access to his females. The demands made upon his testes are not very onerous because the females come into oestrus only once every two years or so, and they have no choice of sexual partner. The male gorilla therefore needs only to manufacture sufficient sperm to ensure that each of his females becomes pregnant with the bare minimum of mating activity. His semen is not of high quality and contains a large proportion of malformed and lethargic sperm.

Chimpanzees are quite different. When the females are ready for sex, their bulbous, flushed behinds advertise the fact and they become utterly promiscuous. For males in search of paternity, every copulation is therefore a gamble. To increase their individual chances of fathering baby chimps, the males have evolved relatively huge testes with a prodigious output of vigorously swimming sperm. Furthermore, the male chimpanzee produces a copious ejaculate to flush out the female's vagina and to overwhelm any sperms inside her from previous trysts.

Relatively speaking, the human male's testes lie midway between those of these two great apes in size and produce semen with a great deal of poor-quality sperms, indicating that men are equipped to combat only moderate levels of sperm competition.

Size for size, some of the largest testes among the vertebrates are found in birds. The record is held by the superb blue fairy wren of Australia, whose testes account for 25 per cent of the body weight. They are polyandrous and the cocks have an especially randy sex life. There is another good reason for male birds being well equipped. Unlike most female mammals, hen birds can store sperm – often for quite long periods – before using it to fertilize their eggs. Stored sperm can be displaced or diluted if a hen mates with another male before her eggs are fertilized. To minimize the risk to their paternity, the cocks of many birds – including sand martins, skylarks and blackbirds – assiduously chaperone their mates, following them everywhere during the period before they start laying when, given the chance, they might copulate again with a strange male. These species have relatively small testes.

However, in other birds, the sexes have to spend time apart during the crucial courtship period. Hen goshawks stay on the nest before laying, conserving their energy while the cocks do all the hunting. In such situations, the males can never be quite sure that their partners have remained faithful. One solution to the problem is frequent copulation, which is the best defence against cuckoldry. Whereas relentless mate-guarders like skylarks copulate only once for every clutch, goshawks are marathon maters, making the sexual connection between 400 and 600 times before the eggs are laid. The explanation of why hens should allow such frequent copulation may be that it increases the male's confidence in his paternity, so that she can rely on his long-term help in raising her brood.

OVERLEAF LEFT
The cloacal kiss of white storks. In some species, like goshawks, couples mate hundreds of times before the eggs appear. Others, such as skylarks, only copulate once or twice.

OVERLEAF RIGHT Sex on a string of mucus. A pair of Australian leopard slugs mating in mid-air. Each is hermaphrodite, and they are exchanging sperm by way of their entwined penises which dangle below their bodies.

Sex at sea – battling against the odds

The watery world is one environment where eggs and sperms can be liberated from the bodies that manufactured them without the tiny cells running the risk of immediate death by desiccation. It is less surprising than it would be in land lovers, therefore, to discover that creatures which live in the open seas and other watery habitats take the battle away from individuals and broadcast their sex cells directly into their surroundings. This activity is known as spawning.

As a sexual strategy, this somewhat stand-off form of reproduction has its risks. The sea, where most spawners live, is an enormous meeting ground and even in a rock pool the task facing a short-lived sperm – that of intercepting an egg of the same species – is formidable indeed. And yet some of the most numerous and widespread creatures in the world are sexual soloists which cast their spawn to the perils of the deep. So in practice the technique must work well enough.

Improving the odds on successful fertilization is a matter of timing and of releasing gametes – reproductive cells of either sex – in numbers which beggar the imagination. A female cod which manages to avoid the nets that sweep the northern seas is capable of making 6 million eggs during a single breeding season. An American oyster does even better. During one session, she sheds a staggering 115 million eggs

and can repeat the performance five or six times during the year. As the oyster population stays more or less the same, it means that for every 700 million eggs released annually during her lifetime, only a couple will survive to replace her and a male when they eventually die. Compared with these odds, it would be easier to win the national lottery several times over. Oysters increase the chances of their sperm and eggs meeting because both sexes tend to settle in beds and synchronize the orgasmic release of their gametes; the females are stimulated to spawn by the 'taste' of an aphrodisiac released by neighbouring males with their milt (sperm).

The tactics adopted by animals such as cod and oysters are fundamental to the process of evolution. No less than for the land lovers described earlier in this chapter, the price of reproductive failure is disastrous, but these marine creatures load the dice in their favour by diverting huge resources to fuel their gonads. Both cod and oyster are nothing more than dedicated egg or sperm factories and their existence revolves around getting enough food to make gametes by the million. In addition, cod are social predators. By living in shoals, they increase their food-finding efficiency; shoaling also helps to co-ordinate the simultaneous release of eggs and sperm. As to whether these fish exercise any choice of spawning partner or indulge in behaviour which enhances the fitness of their offspring, nothing is known. The same applies to the oyster and virtually every other marine animal – much of their lives is still shrouded in mystery.

Many sea creatures with a more settled lifestyle, such as corals, must find a way of getting their timing right if they are to stand a chance of winning the numbers game. Their sedentary habits have enabled them to monopolize suitable shallow shores in the tropics, which guarantee them the strong sunshine needed to power the algae living in their tissues. As individual corals are anchored to their limestone base, synchronous spawning helps them to increase the odds on their gametes meeting. They take their cue from the moon.

Although a quarter of a million miles (400,000 kilometres) away, the moon is still close and large enough to tug powerfully at our planet's watery shawl. The sun's gravity is also sufficiently strong to pluck at the oceans and so lends its support to the pull of the moon. As a consequence, twice each lunar month their combined influence results in surging spring tides for a day or two, flooding the seaboards and ebbing to leave the shores extra high and dry. These very high tides are particularly significant for creatures which breed by spawning, because they rely upon vigorous movements of water to disperse their planktonic embryos and larvae.

One of the most spectacular examples of sexual lunacy takes place annually on Australia's Great Barrier Reef when, for several nights in late spring, countless billions of coral polyps broadcast their spawn in what has been called 'the biggest orgasm on Earth'. During periods of exceptionally high tides, each soft coral polyp ejects a bundle of either eggs or sperm – or both in the case of some hermaphrodite hard corals. Small though these creatures are, the effect of the mass spawning is nothing short of impressive. As the flood tide peaks, visibility around the reefs is severely reduced by a blizzard of tiny capsules floating towards the surface. On their vertical journey, the bundles rupture, releasing their cargoes of gametes.

As there are in the region of two hundred kinds of corals spawning at the same time, it is a miracle that the sperms and eggs meet the right partners in the mêlée. How they achieve this has only recently been discovered. The eggs contain microscopic vesicles – bladder-like sacs – full of a substance that is irresistible to sperm of the same species. Apparently, the surface of the egg is scraped while it is being extruded from the polyp, and this releases the alluring chemicals. After fertilization, a membranous barrier around the eggs prevents the penetration of further sperm.

Many burrowing marine worms trade eggs for energy, and have evolved very active ways of bringing their reduced number of sex cells together. One unusual method is shown by the fireworm.

Flashing fireworms

Those who live in Bermuda are familiar with the luminescent courtship of fireworms (*Odontosyllis enopla*). These are marine cousins of our common garden worms, but their segmented bodies are furnished with a series of hairy paddles for rowing themselves rapidly through the water. For much of the year they live like ordinary worms, scavenging food on the floor of shallow bays, but during their brief spawning periods – usually about an hour after sunset, three days after the full moon – the ripe adults wriggle into the warm surface waters and mate in a flash. Their sexual encounters have the enchantment of a Disneyesque ballet, as they flash and weave trails of stardust in the sea.

When ready to spawn, the females cruise in tight circles, each emitting a bright phosphorescent trail which lasts for only a few seconds. The glow attracts the males, which are smaller than the females and streak up from the bottom with their own lesser 'lights' winking like strobes; they release their sperm alongside the eggs in the female's luminous wake. On a good night, certain bays light up as if by magic. In less than half an hour, the show is over and the worms have returned to the muddy sand from whence they came. All that remains is a myriad of microscopic spheres drifting on the ebb tide, containing the next generation of fireworms.

Such a technique is biologically expensive – the worms are exceedingly active during the event and the production of luminescent mucus takes resources away from the gonads. However, the complex mating behaviour ensures a greater chance that the gametes will meet, and so the worms can risk producing fewer eggs to 'pay' for the energetic nuptials.

In other bristle worms, it is possible to discern advances in anatomical special-izations to reduce the risks of broadcast spawning even further. For instance, palolo worms inhabit the reefs of the Pacific, where the sexes synchronize their spawning without having to leave their crevices. In preparation for their nuptials, the posterior section of each worm is fashioned as a sexual missile or epitoke. It becomes bloated with either sperms or eggs, the paddles become especially broad for swimming and what will eventually be the front develops a rudimentary head complete with eye-spot. When moon and tide dictate that the conditions are just right, the palolos reverse *en masse* from their coral 'burrows' and shake their rear ends free. While the front part of each palolo retreats into the reef to regenerate for another year, the epitokes swim away like 'smart missiles' to mingle with each other and release their contents. In places, they swarm so densely that the sea resembles vermicelli soup – in such circumstances, the gametes can hardly miss each other.

A spawning orgy: millions of squid converge for a frenzy of sex and spawning off the Californian coast. Once the bunches of eggs are laid, the adults die.

There is one planktonic species, of the genus *Autolytus*, that converts its 'tail' into a whole chain of sexual segments which break off and spawn like independent worms. Another, called *Trypanosyllis*, sprouts rosettes of tiny spawning missiles from its rear segment. These have no gut and live only long enough to take part in a bizarre battle of the sexes. When ready to breed, the worms let loose salvos of these sperm- and egg-carriers which behave like self-guided missiles. When they find themselves in the proximity of a 'missile' of opposite sex, they self-destruct, allowing their respective gametes to mix and meet. Fertilization is still an outside event, but swarming greatly enhances the efficiency of the process.

Packaged sex for suckers

In the most advanced members of the mollusc family – the squids and octopuses – one can see the development of increasingly sophisticated behaviour and ingenious accessory organs for overcoming the problems of breeding in the sea. These creatures – especially the squids – are highly active animals and 'burn' a lot of fuel jetting after their fast-moving prey. Using so much energy, the females cannot afford to make thousands

upon thousands of eggs, and accordingly make relatively few, but they have evolved what amounts to a form of internal fertilization. Unlike most of their snail-like relatives, these super-molluscs come in the familiar two sexes and, during the climax of their courtship, the males pass parcels of sperm which 'explode' inside their partners' 'gill chambers'.

There are many kinds of squid, but for one oceanic species – *Loligo opalescens* – certain places off the coast of California are hot spots for sex. They migrate in from the open Pacific in great numbers for what is known as 'the Big Bang' – an orgy of communal mating and egg laying on the seabed. For a short time, the sea seethes with frenetic squid, the males flashing their courtship colours as they woo as many females as possible. The competition for sex is intense. Squid enjoy several mating positions, as the females have alternative sites for the reception and storage of sperm packages. During a full-frontal pass, when a courting couple engages head on in a tangle of tentacles, the male's target is a deep dimple in amongst the female's array of arms, just below her parrot-like beak. However, the male's penis is certainly not up to the job of reaching this receptacle; it is a fairly small papilla – nipple-like protuberance – hidden inside his mantle cavity. The task of transferring the packages of sperm is delegated to a special tentacle called a hectocotylus – the fourth on either the right- or the left-hand side. At the height of the copulatory clinch, the spermatophores (sperm-carrying packages) are extruded into the gill chamber, where they are picked up by the modified mating arm, which then thrusts them into the female's face. As an alternative technique, squid can copulate in parallel, with the male lying alongside the female and entwining his tentacles with hers. In this case, the hectocotyl arm is inserted into the female's mantle cavity and places the gift of sperm parcels close to the opening of the oviduct, where they are strategically located to meet the eggs.

The packages themselves are a marvel of natural technology and behave rather like sperm bombs, bursting when presented to the mate. Again, this may give the donor's sperms a better chance of fertilizing the eggs ahead of those of any males which might follow. Those of *Loligo* are approximately 16 millimetres (just over half an inch) long and shaped rather like a baseball bat. They accumulate in a pouch (called Needham's sac) in the male's reproductive tract, and a large squid can enter the orgy with an arsenal of up to 400. Each one is basically a capped tube enclosing an inner wrapper containing a dense mass of sperm, a blob of cement and a spring-like filament which keeps the whole package under tension. As the spermatophore is withdrawn from the male's genital duct, the lid is loosened and the filamentous spring dislodged. This primes the package, so that by the time it reaches the female, the elastic contraction of the outer capsule causes the contents to be discharged with some force. The cement fixes the structure to one or other of the female's receptacles and, as the mass slowly disintegrates over a period of a day or two, the sperm are liberated.

Manual dexterity is also the key to octopus copulation, except that the mating organ is fashioned out of the third arm on the right. Although the giants of the Pacific North-West are nightmarish monsters – albeit rather gentle ones – the smallest octopods are utterly charming. Among these are little creatures such as *Argonauta*, *Tremoctopus* and *Ocythoe*, which inhabit the warmer regions of the oceans and spend their lives pulsating in the plankton like jellyfish. The males of these pelagic species are exceptionally small; when fully grown, a female *Ocythoe* spans barely 30 centimetres (1 foot), but her opposite number is a mere dwarf which stows away inside the transparent shells of sea tunicates – members of the jelly plankton – after he has eaten them. Despite their diminutive size, each male is extraordinarily well endowed for inseminating his ample mates because he carries a hectocotylus that is enormous in comparison with the rest of his body. This remains coiled inside a pouch on his head, and emerges only when his sex drive is aroused.

OVERLEAF Sex for suckers: cuttlefish in a clinch. A modified mating arm passes a package of sperm into the female under her beak-like mouth.

As the oceans are so vast, the chances of these little pelagic males ever meeting a member of the opposite sex are extremely slim, so they are prepared to 'go for bust' if they are ever so lucky – they can have only one stab at fertilizing some eggs. If the sexes drift to within range of each other, the male withdraws his huge sexual tentacle out of its protective pocket and, clutching a bunch of spermatophores, uses his long reach to insert them into the female's mantle. Its purpose fulfilled, the hectocotylus breaks off. Having shot his single bolt, the male swims away 'emasculated'. For some time, his detached tentacle lashes around near the entrance to the female's oviduct, looking for all the world like a parasitic worm.

In fact, the presence of these strange wriggling things was not always associated with octopod sex. Aristotle was familiar with the eccentric sexual habits of squids and even drew an analogy between the role of the specially constructed mating tentacles and the human penis. But he was not aware of detachable ones. Nor was the eminent French scientist Baron Cuvier more than two millennia later. He examined the thread-like creatures bearing suckers that lingered around the oviducts of female argonauts and concurred with the widely held view of the time that they were parasitic worms; he even christened them *Hectocotylus octopodis*.

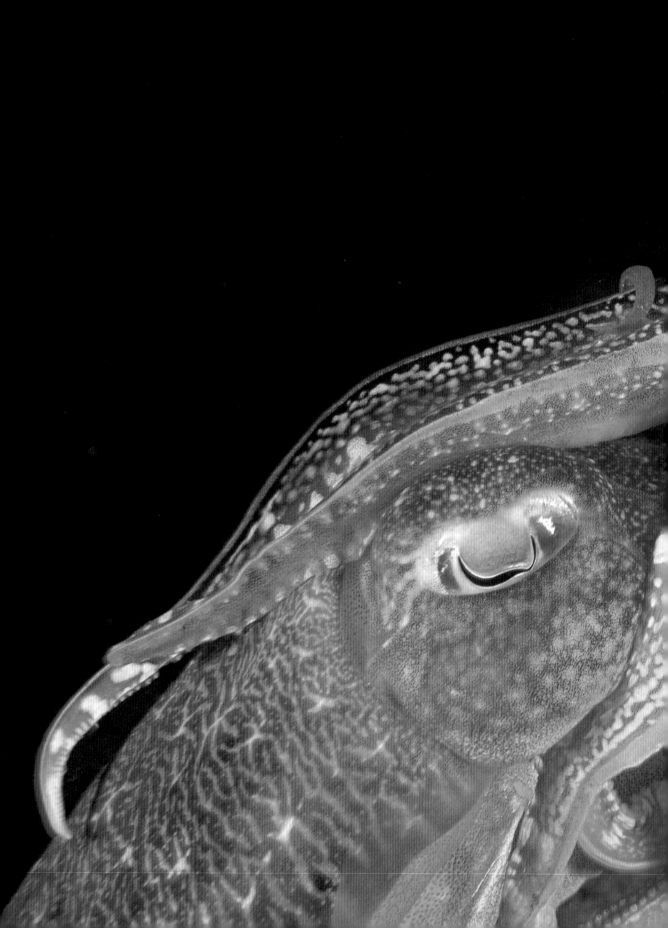

When the truth eventually emerged, the term hectocotylus was retained for the dedicated mating arms of octopuses and squids.

Animals have to make the most of what they have got. In many kinds of fish fins are pressed into service for transferring sperms. Female sharks either nurture their sharklets inside their 'wombs' or lay each of their eggs wrapped in an attractive purse which they snag on to seaweed. Whichever the method used, the eggs must be fertilized internally. Like most fish, sharks of both sexes possess two sets of paired fins equivalent to our arms and legs. In the male, the hind ones are considerably modified into two fleshy rods for copulation. These 'claspers' arise from the edges of the male's cloaca and are grooved on the inside to form open-ended tubes. Stiffened by cartilage, they contain erectile tissue that becomes turgid with blood prior to mating. At the consummation of shark sex, the male coils himself around his mate's body so that one of his extended claspers can enter her cloaca and deliver his sperm.

Other fish, such as the live-bearing toothed carps, have fashioned a mating tube out of the anal fin – the single fin that hangs from the body just behind the vent. Called a gonopodium, it is sometimes quite a splendid structure incorporating a terminal catch and claw mechanism to hook the female by her cloaca – often even tearing her flesh in the process. The guppy has a particularly mobile member, powered by several sets of muscles so that the male can engage with the female whichever side of him she chooses to swim during the sexual act. But, as the name suggests, the one-sided live-bearers are not so flexible because the males have a built-in bias, some anatomically committed to deploying their gonopodia to the right, others only to the left. Luckily, the females are divided into two forms, with their vents partly shielded from one side or the other by scales. Copulation is there-fore possible only between compatible couples – between right-swinging males and left-handed females, and vice versa.

Chastity belts By means of packages or various kinds of extendible organs, males deposit their all-important sperms as close to the eggs as possible. And yet females can be promiscuous in their search for quality males and there are always rivals ready to seize an opportunity to mate. To counteract the danger, the males of some species go to extreme lengths to guarantee their paternity.

In bats, hedgehogs, marsupials and many rodents, the males produce hard-setting seminal fluid. After copulation this blocks the female's vagina, thereby keeping out competing sperms from rivals. Some primates display the same trait. Male murcuri monkeys, which live in the Amazonian rain-forest, pump copious amounts of semen into their females and this coagulates into a conspicuous gelatinous plug. However, the females remain eager for sex and other males learn to winkle the plugs out before copulating. In the case of foxes and of eastern grey squirrels in the USA, the females foil the males' attempts to enforce further chastity by removing the rubbery copulatory plugs themselves within thirty seconds of mating, clearly indicating that there is a conflict between their own sexual agenda and that of the males.

The battle for paternity is wonderfully illustrated by the behaviour of butterflies such as the delicate apollos which drift around alpine pastures and the swallowtails of the genus *Cressida* which grace the flowering vegetation of northern Australia. In these lovely insects, the first male to mate with a virgin female puts paid to her sex life during copulation by secreting a chastity belt called a sphragis around her rear, thus preventing any further intromissions. This desperate strategy is made feasible largely by the female's reproductive anatomy. She has two quite separate openings – one through which the eggs pass and another called the ostium which receives the male's penis and leads to a chamber in which the semen is held temporarily. Sperm gain access to the eggs via an internal passage between the storage chamber and the oviduct. Blocking the ostium therefore does not prevent the female laying eggs, but does ensure that the first male to mate wins the paternity stakes.

The evolution of the sphragis has been one of escalating moves and counter-moves between males and females, each attempting to gain the advantage over the other. Following insemination, males of many butterflies secrete a viscous plug that hardens and more or less seals their partner's orifice. However, as the art of lock-picking flourished in medieval times when padlocks guarded the pudenda of love-lorn maidens, so the males of some butterflies are equipped with a pair of abdominal tweezers for extracting genital bungs, allowing them to supplant sperm from a pre-vious partner. The females of some species have also resisted the males' attempts to enforce celibacy because they derive nutrients from the semen, and so for them promiscuity pays dividends in the form of bigger clutches of eggs. These females have responded to the males' plugs by developing 'externalized' genitalia, sur-rounded by very smooth and glossy plates with the properties of teflon. During copulation, the males could not make their sexual stoppers stick and so the stage was set for the evolution of the ultimate chastity belt – the full sphragis. That of an Australian swallowtail or an apollo is virtually moulded on to and completely girdles the rear of the female's abdomen, and can be removed only with the greatest of difficulty. Furthermore, they often bear long projections that trail beneath the body and act as a deterrent to other sexy males.

LEFT Chastity belt.
In *Cressida* butterflies from
Australia, the male (below)
secretes a girdle around
the end of the female's
abdomen which seals her
up and prevents other
males from subsequently
inseminating her. It is now
a permanent fixture (inset),
thus ensuring the male
fathers all her offspring.

RIGHT Getting in first.
A male passion-vine
butterfly – a Heliconid –
mates with a female as she
emerges from her pupal
case. She hasn't even had
time to inflate her wings.

Bondage

'Sperm wars' favour males which indulge in protracted copulations, because these give their own gametes more time to reach the eggs. Some male crustaceans, such as crabs, keep their mates to themselves by the simple expedient of carrying them around. Breeding isopods and amphipods – shrimp-like creatures which live in both the sea and fresh water throughout the world – swim in tandem, the larger males hanging on to the ripe females by means of specialized gripping legs.

The universal male dilemma of how long to hang on to a mate is highlighted around the warm, moist surface of a cowpat where khaki-coloured flies copulate. The males congregate in such apparently insalubrious places because this is where the females deposit their eggs. Given the chance, a female takes a succession of males, but the last one fathers about 70 per cent of her eggs. When a mature female arrives in the vicinity, she is quickly mounted by a male and flown a metre (yard) or two away from the cowpat to be inseminated. But she will remain available for sex until she has finished laying her clutch. The male therefore has a choice: to ride her and see off other males until she turns frigid – although by doing so, he will miss other mating opportunities – or to abandon her and face losing potential progeny if she consents to sex with another partner. With dung flies, there is such competition for females that natural selection has favoured a compromise, with males clinging for a while after ejaculating, thereby discouraging take-over bids, although they perhaps lose a few extra matings.

Many animals spend far longer than is strictly necessary simply to transfer semen. A male house-fly needs about fifteen minutes to impregnate a female, but copulation generally lasts for an hour – the male takes the extra time to guard his investment while his partner is still sexually motivated. Mating moths and butterflies stay tied together for a day, while male locusts often stay mounted for two. This pales into insignificance when compared with male weevils belonging to the species *Rhytirrhinus surcoufi*; they have been recorded as staying on the backs of their mates for a month without losing contact, thus imposing a kind of monogamy on the females.

Among the vertebrates, male frogs can be equally dedicated when it comes to clinging for a long time, and may embrace and so guard their gravid partners for days in order not to miss the strings of eggs. The males of the African toad called *Breviceps* – a small desert toad – even stick themselves to the rumps of their relatively huge mates with glue secreted from their chests.

Sexual ties of a different nature are practised by members of the dog family. Among wolves, for instance, which are the wild precursors of our domesticated pets, bitches in heat have a magnetic appeal for all males in the pack. But copulation during the female's most fertile period is the prerogative of the top male and a technique has evolved which ensures that it is his pups and not anyone else's which appear two months later. After insertion, the tip of the male's penis swells up, making withdrawal temporarily impossible. To begin with, the couple proceed in the normal mating position with the male perched up behind the female. After a minute or so he usually dismounts, throws a leg over his trapped penis and turns to face away from the bitch. The two then stand around like a pair of Siamese twins joined by their bottoms. While they are intimately bonded for perhaps half an hour, the sperms have time to wriggle some way up the female's reproductive tract. Should a lesser male subsequently mount her, his sperms have a much reduced chance of reaching any of the eggs first.

Dirty tactics

Aedes aegypti is one of the most notorious mosquitoes in the world, because egg-bound females carry the malignant virus responsible for yellow fever throughout tropical Africa and America. Deadly though they may be, one aspect of their sex life is fascinating. Once the female *Aedes* has been impregnated, her drive to mate vanishes. The males are responsible for the sudden mood swing because their semen contains a hormone which is rapidly absorbed through the vaginal walls into the female's nervous circuitry and switches off her urge to mate. As a sexual sedative, the substance is exceptionally potent; a sample taken from one male is sufficient to make over sixty females utterly frigid.

Monogamy in Heliconid butterflies is also a matter of chemistry. These eye-catching insects, their velvet-black wings lavishly decorated with splashes of red, yellow and orange, live in the American tropics, where they brazenly expose themselves in forest glades. They can afford to flaunt themselves because their juicy bodies are protected by poison – a fact that birds ignore at their peril. Not only do the butterflies have a nauseating taste, they also emit a filthy stench if they are molested. The males have a wonderful sense of smell and can readily determine the sex of an individual contained within a chrysalis by its scent. If it promises to be a virgin female and competition from other males is fierce, a male Heliconid will guard the pupal case and waft an offensive scent emanating from a pair of 'stink clubs' on the tip of his abdomen to smother the female's erotic perfume. This 'anaphrodisiac' repulses rivals and allows the male to copulate with the female as soon as she breaks out, even before her wings are expanded. While mating on the empty chrysalis, the male Heliconid continues to kill his lover's sex appeal by showering her with his own offensive stink and so deters other males from copulating with her and displacing his sperm. This dirty trick may not be in the female's interest – she might be best served by encouraging sperm competition – so why she consents to be made to smell vile is far from clear; perhaps a newly impregnated female gains by not wasting time on further 'unnecessary' copulations.

Getting in first

Such are the reproductive rewards for males of being the first to impregnate females that those of a few species are genetically primed to have sex with barely mature partners. As already described, male Heliconid butterflies are under such pressure and, in 42 per cent of the species, even insert the tips of their abdomens into the chrysalids to make sexual contact with the virgin female inside. In the bee *Centris pallida*, which lives in the deserts of the USA, the grubs pupate in the soil. The drones are the first to hatch and spend the early mornings when the air is still, cruising a few centimetres (an inch or two) above the ground until they catch the scent of a fresh queen. On sensing the erotic aroma, the male tumbles on to the spot where the perfume is strongest and hurls back the loose rubble with his forelegs to unearth the virgin bee. Without a moment to lose, he clutches her and flies off to the nearest bush to copulate.

The males of some mosquitoes act as 'midwives', easing young females out of their pupal cases with a pair of abdominal forceps. Once the fully formed but somewhat crumpled female is extricated, the male promptly mates with her.

As with the Heliconids, sex is taken into the pupal case in *Orygia splendida*, a moth related to the gypsy moth. The male is normal looking with a pair of pretty wings, but the female is dowdy. In fact she never really grows up, because she becomes fertile as a grub when still imprisoned in her cocoon. Without ever emerging into the light of day, she attracts a male to her by her irresistible smell. When a male alights, his exciting body odour stimulates her to claw a hole in her cocoon, which allows him to mate. Afterwards, he flies off to find another moth Lolita, while she lays her eggs and dies without setting foot outside.

Sex takes place in the nursery even in stoats. During the summer, males are combing the countryside not only for prey, but also for nests containing young virgin stoats. On finding one, the male forcibly inseminates her, even though she protests vigorously and may well be so young that her eyes are closed.

Bizarre though such behaviour appears, it is but one of the outcomes of the fierce pressures that males are under to mate in a hurry to ensure their genes live on. The females themselves may benefit because their sons will indulge in the same behaviour and successfully propagate their genes.

Poisonous semen

Fruit-flies provide the ultimate expression of warfare between sexes – the males, in attempting to control their mates chemically, poison them while the females search frantically for antidotes. The discovery came to light when it was noticed that highly promiscuous female flies were short-lived. This was due not to the undoubted strain of egg production, but to a surfeit of sex. Further investigation revealed that the seminal fluid was the culprit, leading the females to an early grave. Semen is not just a medium for transporting sperm; it is a cocktail of secretions, some of which affect the female's behaviour, usually to the male's benefit. As we have already discussed, some insect testes manufacture proteins which improve

the male's chances of paternity by reducing his mate's libido after copulation. Other chemicals stimulate her to lay her eggs sooner rather than later. This is the kind of molecular control exercised by male fruit-flies attempting to realize a quick return on their reproductive investment, and has resulted in a molecular 'arms race'. Female fruit-flies have counter-attacked their mates' actions with their own chemical antidotes, favouring the males with more powerful compounds to which they have no answer. Sex has become murder. Now, to enhance his chances of fathering offspring by advancing ovulation, the male fruit-fly produces seminal fluid so 'strong' that it is toxic and prematurely poisons the female, but not before she has laid her eggs.

For the males of species in which the females are born killers, mating is *Suicidal sex* a dangerous proposition. Having delivered their sperm, some males appear to make the supreme sacrifice – and end up as meals. And yet, such suicidal tactics make sense in the context of sperm wars, especially if the males are unlikely to have more than one stab at breeding. There is little point in a male escaping with his life if his paternity is not assured. If, by commiting suicide during sex, he keeps his savage partner occupied while his, and not someone else's, gametes seek hers, the sacrifice pays off.

One of the best-known dangerous liaisons is forged by male praying mantises. The 1800 or so species include some of the most striking-looking insects in the world, but their beauty belies their nature. These deadly predators hunt by stealth, snatching insects and small lizards with a lightning flick of their spiked forelimbs. Sadly for the males, the large females are capable of delivering the ultimate 'love bite'; they tend to be sexual cannibals and treat their mates as prey. After copulation, the males attempt to escape, but in some species they fail. Starting with his head, the female munches through her mate's body while his abdomen automatically completes the business of transferring a packet of sperm into her genital opening. The male's body is the ultimate nuptial gift, because by consuming her partner the female is able to produce significantly more eggs. She therefore benefits from her macabre habits, but so does he – he literally gives his all and, as a consequence, fathers more offspring.

Lethal love-bite. A female praying mantis has devoured the head of the male yet his body continues mating. He loses his life but his paternity is ensured.

Male spiders always face the risk of being devoured when they consummate their courtship, but male red-backs appear to be the only ones which positively commit suicide during sex. Red-backs are one of Australia's most venomous and most feared spiders. Unfortunately, they often live uncomfortably close to human dwellings, where the warmth and light attracts a continuous supply of insects into their conical webs. As is normal for spiders, the sexes are so different that they might belong to separate species; the female is about seven times larger than her suitors and sports a sinister red stripe running down her back.

The diminutive male is understandably cautious about entering a female's silken lair. He spends two or more hours arousing her sexual interest by abseiling into her web and plucking and tapping a message of intent on the individual threads. She signals her acquiescence by doing nothing to prevent his approach. At last he makes contact and crawls on to the underside of her relatively enormous body to indulge in a little foreplay. After 'mouthing' her genital orifice, he uncoils the charged end of one of his palps – his sexual organ – and places it inside her, at the same time discharging it of the semen it contains.

So far, so good. But then the male suddenly somersaults through 180 degrees and places his abdomen squarely between the female's murderous fangs. This she certainly cannot ignore, and invariably she impales him. The first strike is not usually lethal, because the male attempts to mate again, discharging his second palp into her before making another determined somersault, this time into the jaws of death. The fully inseminated female now bites him in earnest, injects tissue-liquefying venom and sucks his body dry. But his sperm live on inside her body, ready to fertilize her eggs.

Other remarkable strategies have evolved which illustrate the extremes to which males will go to give their own sperm the best chance of reaching the eggs first. In Australia, male red-tailed phascogales – small, squirrel-like carnivores – burn themselves out in an all-or-nothing quest for fatherhood. These endearing little marsupials have a short but exhausting mating season during the southern spring, which leaves the males wrecked. They are intensely territorial and supremely com-petitive, chasing up and down trees and racing in and out of hollows searching for females. The female phascogales are extremely shy and make the males court them energetically before submitting to prolonged and vigorous sex. So intent are the males on finding as many targets as possible for their precious sperm that they have no time to feed during their week of frenzied sexual activity. While the freshly impregnated females retire to their nests, the knackered males rapidly succumb to a combination of infections, failed livers, gut ulcers, extensive haemorrhages and extreme weight loss. These symp-toms accompany a rise in the level of their blood cortico-steroids and a catastrophic suppression of their immunological system – characteristics of severe stress. Not one adult male survives. But 50 per cent of the females' babies will be males and by the following spring they will be mature enough to enter the same lethal sexual arena.

The egg is now fertilized – in a split second, a new life has been initiated. This has been achieved against astronomical odds. Both the sperm and its slave, the male body which produced it and propelled it into the female's tract, have had to be supreme players in

One battle over, another looms

the most rigorous and demanding contest on earth – survival. The male has relied on countless brawling ancestors, themselves winners endowed with the skills needed to overcome both physical dangers and cut-throat competition from rivals. His sperm has passed the female's demanding tests for quality control. Of the billions that started the race, many were deformed, most simply got lost or died of exhaustion. Of the few that lashed their way to the egg, only one was victorious. On arriving at its destination, it began a complex sequence of chemical code-breaking whereby enzymes – special proteins – in the tip of its head unlocked the egg's surface and allowed the sperm to enter its protoplasm. In a fraction of a second, a miraculous transformation took place in the composition of the cell, enabling the egg to shut out all other sperms which subsequently attempted to pierce it. Once safely inside, the sperm casts off its tail, leaving only the head, packed with the male's genes, his sole contribution to the new offspring.

The sheer complexity of what follows defies the imagination. If there be miracles, then the defining moment of one was when the hereditary instructions of both male and female were collated in the fusion of egg and sperm nuclei and a new life was conceived in a flurry of membranes and rapidly dividing cells. Although it takes place on a microscopic scale, this is the key event over which the sexes have been striving to exert control.

However, the share each parent has in that new individual is already unequal – the sperm donates only its genes to the relatively massive egg. For the time being, it seems, the male has got away with the smaller down payment. But now a fresh conflict looms – over the question of parental care. The mother would prefer to go on and produce more eggs, and the father to spread his sperm around more females. Nevertheless, conception does not end the 'costs' of reproduction for all creatures. For many, a great deal of effort will have to be expended on caring for their offspring. And who does that is very much decided by yet another dispute between the sexes.

The PARENTAL DILEMMA

T he battles that drive a wedge between the sexes in the business of mating are just as apparent in parenting. Although mothers and fathers caring for their offspring might present a picture of cosy co-operation, both parents in fact suffer from a severe conflict of interests. On the one hand, each needs to ensure the survival of his or her offspring – otherwise the whole effort of reproduction will have been wasted. On the other hand, a male or female who spends time guarding eggs or supporting a family may be less successful in the reproductive stakes than one who opts out of the responsibility and continues to breed with other partners. There are also other disincentives to parenting. In defending its family against predators, an adult is in danger of being killed, and by devoting time to feeding it, the parent will probably spend less time feeding itself – which, in the long run, may mean producing fewer offspring.

PREVIOUS PAGES
Left holding the baby.
A female Californian sea-lion
raises her pup as a single
mother. She mated with the
father during the previous
season and might not have
seen him since.

Males have a greater opportunity and motivation to play fast and loose as parents because, as we have seen, their prolific supply of sperm makes it easier for them to make more offspring with multiple partners. By contrast, females invest heavily in reproduction in the form of big eggs or energy-draining pregnancies. Over the course of evolution females appear to have been unhappy with this disparity, and across the animal kingdom it is possible to see ways and means by which they have attempted to counter the male's potential for maverick behaviour and bring him back into the parental fold. Nevertheless, the aim of reproduction is to generate the maximum number of surviving offspring for the least effort. Therefore males continue to take a chance and philander – arguably that is a fundamental characteristic of male behaviour – so a vigorous tussle continues between the sexes over how the burden of parenthood is to be shared, or whether it is to be shared at all. At stake behind all the manoeuvring is the survival of the next generation, the loss of which neither sex can afford.

The chick from hell

Even the most impressive examples of parental devotion are the outcome of sexual selfishness. An especially noteworthy one is provided by pairs of wandering albatrosses, which nest on small, desolate islands close to the Antarctic Circle; their apparently selfless dedication to their chicks and their mutual fidelity are not what they seem.

A female wandering albatross fidgets on her nest on top of a clump of tussock grass on the island of South Georgia and cranes her head forward to inspect what is happening to the egg beneath her belly. She laid it on Christmas Day and since then she and her mate have unfailingly taken turns to keep it warm. Now, seventy days later, in early March, their commitment is starting to pay off as a blind, wet, vulnerable little chick struggles free from the shell inside which it has safely completed the first stage of its development. Although a stiff wind chilled by the icy sea ruffles the mother's feathers, beneath her breast the chick snuggles up against her naked brood patch and luxuriates in the heat derived from her body. After a while, the warmth drives out the dampness from its coat and infuses the chick with the energy to beg. The mother obliges by squirting a little oil and liquid stomach contents into its gape. But her faithful partner is soon on hand, returning with a crop full of food after a thirty-six-hour foraging trip far out to sea.

Together, the pair of wanderers appear to be the epitome of parental perfection in the animal world. They are imbued with such a powerful instinct to look after their single chick that they often squabble over which of them will take the next duty to care for the little creature. This strong parental drive is crucial because they must spend the next ten months of their lives commuting between the open ocean and their nest site, provisioning their offspring if it is to stand any chance at all of fledging. Such a long period of dependency is forced upon these great albatrosses by the difficulties of catching squid – which make up the vast majority of their diet – in the Antarctic Ocean. The sheer distances each adult has to travel and the time it takes to find prey mean that a single bird could never supply the ravenous youngster with enough food to enable it to endure the cruel southern winter ahead.

Wandering albatrosses are the jumbos among flying sea-birds – the flightless emperor penguin is heavier – and their size accounts for their success. Only such large birds could have the range and speed to rove the vast southern oceans for food, alighting on remote sub-Antarctic islands to nest. For their young, fledging from these windswept breeding sites and launching into a lifestyle like that of their parents is a challenge. To survive in the demanding ocean wilderness, they have to be to all intents and purposes 'adults'. The parents are therefore condemned to rear their chick from a hatching weight of 80 grams (3 ounces) to an 8-kilogram (18-pound) fledgling – a hundredfold increase. But this is not all. By mid-winter, the wanderer's gargantuan chick resembles a pot-bellied, furry bowling skittle, standing a metre (over 3 feet) tall and weighing 35 kilograms (80 pounds), incredibly three times as much as its father; it is nothing more than a down-covered stomach surmounted by a beak. The store of fat will eventually fuel its transition to independence.

In evolving large size, the wandering albatross has sentenced itself to rearing huge offspring, and such are the difficulties in doing this successfully that not only

Both parents shackled:
a wandering albatross chick
exacts a punishing schedule
of feeding on both of its
parents. It will only survive if
both its mother and father
bring it food. The adult
above is a male.

have they reduced their clutch size to one, they have gone one step further and reduced their frequency of breeding. They are the only group of birds to have a cycle of nesting that extends over two years – the hens lay one egg every other year. The wanderer has effectively saddled itself with 'a chick from hell', empowered by its genes to grow into one of the largest flying birds on Earth. In doing so, it demands from its parents over 1.5 kilograms (3 pounds) of food per day, all of which has to be caught in the turbulent, featureless oceans by means of learned skills and impressive stamina.

The fidelity of the parent wanderers – one pair is known to have stayed together for forty years – is forged not out of altruistic consideration for each other, but out of a combination of environmental circumstances and self-interest. The chick shackles the parents to an endurance exercise comparable to any athletic feat on earth, and the adults have no choice but to submit to the innate demands of their offspring. For wandering albatrosses, single parenthood is simply not an option – lone birds fail wholesale when, through accident or death, their partners do not return with food for the nestling. The mammoth chick, together with the challenging environment in which the adults have to forage, force the male and female into that ultimate alliance of co-operation and faithfulness – absolute monogamy.

As we shall see, the ways in which conflicts of interests between males and females have been resolved have generated

Uncaring parents

a whole spectrum of parental relationships. However, in the majority of animals, the adults have no 'after-sale service' agreement with their offspring!

Few creatures which live in water have evolved a method of containing their eggs and offspring so that they can be managed in a manner which aids their survival. Once the females have jettisoned them into their surroundings, the young are on their own. Perhaps guarding eggs and fry floating in the mighty ocean is too difficult. A whole range of marine invertebrates and fish therefore play a ruthless game of roulette with their offspring, reducing their parental care to zero and putting all their effort into producing astronomical numbers of gametes (reproductive cells). As a consequence, during the spring and summer, the surfaces of seas around the globe are a maelstrom of glistening eggs and weird and wonderfully shaped immature forms of hydroids, worms, crustaceans, sea urchins, molluscs and fish.

Such unimaginable numbers result from a reproductive strategy which is diametrically opposite to that of the wandering albatross. In the race to outbreed others, each female manufactures as many eggs as possible so that her own offspring will overwhelm those of her competitors. But inevitably, for the millions of eggs which many spawners produce (see Chapter 3), survival is a lottery

BELOW Fending for themselves, the fertilized eggs (left) and larval forms of many sea creatures like lobsters (right) are left to their own devices. The careless parents invest in sheer numbers to maintain their line.

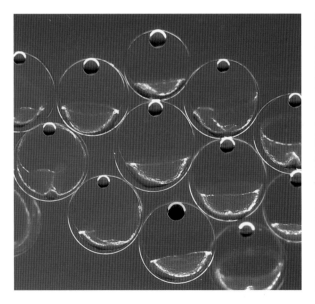
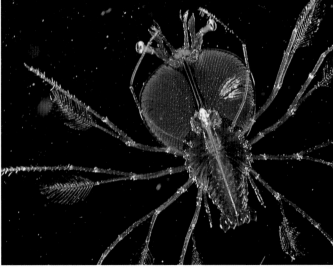

as most of them will perish in the plankton – the vast population of tiny creatures and plants that drifts near the surface of the ocean – and be consumed by many kinds of predators. However, the evolutionary gamble that an uncaring parent takes is that a few of her multitudinous offspring will escape a premature death and carry on the line.

There are exceptions in which marine species have evolved a rudimentary form of parental behaviour to give their eggs or offspring a better chance of life. Black damsel fish, for example, exhibit a rudimentary form of caring. Inhabiting the Indo-Pacific reefs, these dusky little fish corral their fry like sheepdogs, presumably guarding them against a host of enemies which would otherwise speedily snap them up. In this species and in many other fish which have evolved parental behaviour, it is the males which tend to be landed with the brood.

Male guardians

The sea is an incomprehensibly vast volume of water and those fish which have evolved a system of parental care tend to be shallow-water dwellers, associated with reefs where the communities are relatively crowded. In such places, there may be a greater exposure to predators, hence the desirability of some form of parenting.

During the act of spawning, the female firstly releases the eggs close to the male so that he can shed his sperm over them. If she then makes a hasty retreat, the male has no choice but to guard them, otherwise the eggs will be eaten and both will lose out. He is, as it were, left holding the clutch. The order in which spawning takes place might explain why so many egg attenders among fishes are males. The sergeant-major fish is one such species.

Recognized by their vertical black stripes on a yellowish background, sergeant-majors are common inhabitants of tropical reefs throughout the world, where they feed in company with other species in the upper layers of the plankton. During the afternoons when they are ready to breed, the males assume a deep bluish courting coloration and each claims a site along the edge of a coral wall which it scrapes clean with its mouth while violently fanning the water. Within half an hour of establishing a little breeding community, the males begin to solicit passing females by swimming towards them in a zig-zag fashion and abruptly diving back to their nests. Gravid female passers-by follow the males down to their territories and they form into pairs. After a brief courtship, spawning is accomplished with much tail-trembling and head-to-tail circling. Having fertilized one batch of eggs, the male continues to entertain new partners until he has accumulated a dense mass of perhaps 200,000 eggs which he dare not leave for a moment. For four days and nights, he has to clean and guard the nest and aggressively chase away all other fishes which would otherwise make a meal out of his prized eggs. When the fry appear, they swim for cover between the long spines of pin-cushion sea urchins, thus relieving the male of his parental responsibilities.

Fresh water rarely runs deep, and the fish which live in rivers and lakes often display much interesting parental care. In the cichlids which inhabit the lakes of Africa's Great Rift Valley, the males have managed to shift the burden of parenthood back to the females. Their spawning rituals are variations on a theme and include a kind of oral sex for ensuring fertilization. Once the female has jettisoned her eggs in response to her partner's flamboyant courtship, she spins around and appears to eat them while the male sprinkles his sperm over them. However, females are sometimes so quick off the mark that there is a serious risk of them taking the spawn into their capacious mouths before all the eggs are fertilized. Accordingly, the males of several species retain the female's interest by flagging their anal fin, on which there are egg-like patterns. In *Haplochromis burtoni*, for instance, the male has a series of golden 'egg spots' which he flashes in front of his mate's snout while he ejaculates. She seems to be deceived by these roundels and grabs at them as though they were real eggs, but all she gets is a mouthful of milt, conveniently mixing the sperms with any unfertilized eggs.

The relationship between the sexes is not continued. The male is free to find more mates while the female is burdened with a mouthful of spawn which she keeps hidden from egg thieves and maintains in a well-oxygenated stream of water passing through her gills. Ultimately, when the eggs hatch, she allows the fry to take shelter between her jaws – at least for a short time. For her, this period of oral motherhood is draining as she is prevented from feeding and breeding again until her offspring have outgrown their nursery.

There is one group of fish in which the conventional sexual roles appear to be so completely 'reversed' that the males become true mothers. By any reckoning seahorses are strange creatures. With a head resembling the knight in a game of chess, scanning their surroundings with independently moving eyes, a body encased in armour, a prehensile tail, with only a single fin used for propulsion, they hardly look like fish at all. However, the oddest thing about them is that the males uniquely become pregnant!

Ranging across the coastal waters of the tropics and warmer temperate regions, the thirty-five kinds of seahorse vary from thumb-sized 'sea ponies' which live in the Gulf of Mexico to the 35-centimetre (14-inch) giants of the eastern Pacific. All show the same kind of breeding arrangement, with the males becoming enslaved by the females to look after the young. No male animal is known to lavish greater care on his offspring. Only pipe fishes, which are closely related to seahorses, have such specialized paternal behaviour, although they do not all show the same degree of pouch development.

After a protracted period of courtship in which both male and female change colour, the gravid female seahorse presses her belly against her partner's, inserts what looks like a penis – her ovipositor – into the brood pouch on his abdomen and offloads her eggs into it. Exhausted, she then plays no further part in the process, but swims away to maximize her breeding opportunities by growing another batch of eggs. The male's freedom is severely curtailed while he takes on the role of mother but, by his devotion, he improves the survival chances of their joint family. Once safely protected inside his pouch, the eggs are not only fertilized but take over their father's body by embedding in the walls of the chamber which, like a placenta,

RIGHT A devoted dad. The male short-snouted seahorse guards his babies in his brood pouch. He has a pseudo-pregnancy complete with labour and birth.

BELOW A mother's precious mouthful. This female cichlid from Lake Tanganyika keeps her brood in her mouth for safe keeping. The father takes no interest in his fry.

is richly serviced with blood vessels to supply the embryos with oxygen and nutrients. Even when they have hatched, the tiny 'sea foals' stay for a time inside the male's nursery, where they continue to be nourished by secretions from the pouch. Amazingly, the production of these is stimulated by prolactin, one of the hormones of mammalian pregnancy. After a month or so, depending upon the temperature, the male goes into labour, expressing his tiny free-swimming fry into the sea with contractions of his greatly swollen pouch. The process may take two days and brings to an abrupt end his current bout of motherhood.

It is difficult to escape the comparison between the seahorse's 'pregnancy' and that of a mother mammal. Indeed, so similar are they that one might think that pregnant seahorses were really females, were it not for the fact that the individuals which care for the brood produce wriggling, motile sperm.

This raises the question of how female seahorses and their kin managed to achieve such a degree of parental emancipation. The answer probably lies in their phenomenal degree of specialization. These weird creatures cower among stands of eel grass, behaving in a truly inconspicuous manner. Anchored to the fronds, they barely move except to suck up morsels of drifting food through their tubular mouths. Little energy flows through their bodies, and this means that there is little to spare for making offspring. The male is therefore forced to share the costs of reproduction or else none of the babies would survive. In these extraordinary fishes, the male probably devotes just as many resources to nourishing the embryos as his mate does in forming the eggs in the first place. The females have therefore well and truly brought the males back into the parental fold.

Frog fathers Even among the amphibians which care for their young, single-parent fathers are frequently the norm. In fish, parental care appears to be a defensive ploy to ward off egg-eaters. However, in the tailless amphibians – frogs and toads – there is a logistical problem in parenting insofar as the adults and their offspring inhabit entirely different worlds; the eggs and tadpoles are fully aquatic, whereas the adults spend their lives on land except when they are spawning. Once they have mated in the water, most frogs and toads abandon their unprotected eggs to their fate. The odds against an individual offspring's survival are incredible; only one in 10,000 eggs needs to achieve adulthood in order to maintain the status quo. The females bear the huge metabolic cost of the wastage by 'choosing' to forsake their offspring in order to conquer the land – and, judging by the number of these amphibians there are on Earth, it is a very viable strategy. Nevertheless, about one in every ten of the 3500 kinds of frogs and toads do exhibit some degree of caring behaviour, which varies according to the precise circumstances in which the individual species live. Observation suggests that many parental battles rage in frogdom.

In African bullfrogs, for example, it is the pugilistic males which care for both the spawn and the tadpoles. These frogs are explosive breeders, stimulated into a sexual frenzy by the first heavy summer rains. Compared with the females of the species, the males are enormous, aggressive, sporting a pair of vicious fangs in their lower jaws and giving vent to ear-splitting croaks which sound like football fans' rattles. By battling, the largest ones establish territories in shallow water and fertilize the eggs of the succession of females which visit them. But, unlike many other amphibians, African bullfrogs face a serious problem; as they spawn in temporary pools or in the shallow edges of larger bodies of water, they are very vulnerable to their watery nurseries drying up. If the frogs simply left their eggs, few if any tadpoles would survive, so some form of parental attendance is necessary.

The job of guarding the eggs is left entirely to the hefty males. With several batches of spawn amounting to thousands of eggs, they have a powerful incentive to stay and protect them. Foraging birds and snakes are given short shrift by the aggressive frogs, but the chief danger comes from the withering heat of the tropical sun, which drives up the water temperature and relentlessly shrinks the pools. Once the eggs hatch, the male bullfrog shepherds his shoal of tadpoles like a well-trained border collie with a flock of sheep. If the water gets too hot, he drives them into deeper and thus cooler water. In the event of his nursery beginning to dry up, he uses his snout and forelegs to excavate a channel to a neighbouring puddle, which may flood into his own domain or, failing that, acts as an escape route for his offspring.

Some of the tadpoles are equipped to survive a rapid drying out of their surroundings. About 10 per cent of them are substantially larger than the majority and change into little air-breathing froglets which can emerge on to the land well ahead of the rest. However, the survival of most of the brood largely depends on the extent of the male's devotion to his paternal role.

Many frogs and toads, which show some degree of egg attendance and concern for their tadpoles, live in the hot but humid forests of the tropics. In such places they have evolved techniques of reproducing out of water, thus removing the major impediment to a close association between them and their offspring. Sometimes the relationship is astonishingly intimate. There can scarcely be a less suitable place to brood eggs than in the acid-secreting stomach and yet there is in Australia a very

Fatherhood in frogdom. A male glass frog from Belize (top) guards his potential offspring, and a reticulated poison dart frog (inset) from Peru takes his tadpoles to water.

rare frog called *Rheobatrachis silus* in which the female swallows the eggs. All her gastric activity ceases for several weeks, after which she vomits the young out into the world. A similar form of internal brooding is practised by the males of a tiny frog discovered by Charles Darwin in southern Chile. When the females have laid their eggs, the males appear to ingest them, but in fact they are taken into his unusually capacious vocal sac. There they develop until they are ready to jump out of their father's mouth.

The arrow poison frogs of Central America have made the leap from aquatic spawning to laying terrestrial eggs. The males are left guarding them until they hatch, fiercely protecting them from egg thieves, cleaning potential pathogens such as fungi from their surfaces and, most importantly of all, keeping the clutch moist, often by voiding the contents of their bladders over it. When the eggs hatch, it is the father's business to transport the tadpoles on his back to a stream or to one of the small pools of water that accumulate in the centres of bromeliads. The females of some species contribute to the welfare of their young by paying frequent visits to these nurseries and depositing infertile eggs into the miniature pools as food for their tadpoles. In the so-called marsupial frogs, the females are full-time mothers. During their sexual embrace, the male shoves the eggs into special pouches on the female's back, where they are protected and nourished during the course of their development.

In the little whistling frog of Guyana, the balance of advantage over who looks after the brood shifts backwards and forwards between the sexes. The males are committed fathers only when the forest is fairly dry. Under these conditions, fertile females are few and far between. So if a male is lucky enough to have mated, his best option is to take great care of the eggs by staying with them until they hatch. He will even fight his mate for the privilege of doing so, somewhat unromantically banishing her from the cavity in which she has deposited them. But the male's tactics change when wetter conditions prevail. Then, with plenty of gravid females around, he abandons all notions of fatherhood and becomes a playboy, making a quick exit as soon as he has fertilized the eggs. The female is left with no choice but to guard them herself.

In becoming faithful egg-sitters, male frogs and toads undoubtedly lose further mating opportunities. With a batch of eggs to brood and keep moist, the male becomes dumb and no longer sings for sex. The advantage to the female frogs is clear – they can lay further clutches, perhaps as many as six during the course of a year – but the male appears to be greatly handicapped in this version of the generation game. However, this impression is misleading. The benefits to brooding males have been estimated for a noisy brown tree frog that lives in the rain forests of Puerto Rico. Known as *el coqui* because of its voice, each male *Eleutherodactylus coqui* guards the thirty or so eggs laid by his mate until they hatch. Experimental removal of the males has revealed how necessary they are in ensuring the survival of the brood. Whereas over three quarters of the guarded clutches hatched, rather less than a quarter of the abandoned ones did so. In the latter cases, the chief causes of egg mortality were desiccation and cannibalism by other frogs of the same species. The eggs take three weeks to develop, and during this period the male probably loses the chance to mate with one additional female. By sacrificing this single bout of sex in favour of loyally guarding one brood at a time, he generates far more offspring than he would if he used any other combination of parental care and abandonment.

Internal fertilization: back to mother care

Sperm and eggs are completely aquatic forms of life. If they are abandoned on terra firma, their endurance is measured in seconds, or minutes at the most. For those animals which emerged from the water to take advantage of the bountiful resources of the land, reproduction involved a fresh set of very challenging problems. Foremost among them was the mechanism for bringing sperms and eggs together inside the body – a necessary prerequisite of a fully terrestrial existence, as explained in Chapter 3. The inherently large size of the eggs made them difficult objects to transfer, and so it was the male gametes which made the running into the female's body. This increasingly put the initial onus of parenthood on the female, because once males had delivered their sperms, they could clear off and seek other mates.

Internal fertilization is practised by many arthropods – especially insects and spiders – and this enabled them to conquer the land hundreds of millions of years before our back-boned ancestors slithered from the primeval swamps. The spiders were early inhabitants, and today the females of many species remain the sole carers. Most people would regard the pink-footed tarantula as a nightmarish creature. The size of an outstretched hand and covered with a pile of irritating hairs, this so-called bird-eating spider is one of the giants of its kind. Despite its appearance, however, it is fairly harmless to humans; in the Amazon jungle where it lurks, it captures insects, small mammals and perhaps the occasional nestling. Females are bigger than males – it is in their reproductive interests to be large so that they can produce as many eggs as possible. Size is of less importance to the males. The palps which were once used for feeding are altered for injecting sperm during their final moult and so the males slowly starve to death during the year or so when they are sexually active. Their immediate problem is to escape from the females after mating so that they can pursue more sexual partners.

Once she has mated, the female tarantula temporarily gives up the life of a roving hunter, and lays between 500 and 1000 eggs into a silken cocoon, which she guards either by resting her front feet on it or by squatting over it like a brooding hen. Should anything come too close to her and her cocoon, she spreads her enormous glistening fangs, which she does not hesitate to use if seriously provoked. After a week or two, her vigil is rewarded by the appearance of the spiderlings.

Once the male spider has inseminated the female and so done his best to guarantee his paternity (see Chapter 3), he is free to vanish. But why does his mate allow him to get away with sentencing her to become a lone mother? The answer is tied up in the fate of her sons. The female will tolerate being abandoned if her male offspring will, in turn, become more profligate breeders by leaving their mates after copulation. They will, after all, be carrying her genes and if by behaving like their philandering father they help to spread more of them, then it pays the female tarantula to be a single parent. Environmental factors also pitch in to nudge the relationship between the parents one way or the other: in lush tropical forests where there is plenty of prey for the female to catch and devour, a mother tarantula can just 'afford' to lose her mate. The balance is a fine one, because during the period when she is guarding her brood, she often comes critically close to starving. On some occasions, she has to opt for self-preservation and abandon her brood in favour of feeding herself – after all, she can always breed again.

Being saddled with the babies, the females of some spiders make amazingly good mothers. They assiduously guard their egg sacs and when the spiderlings appear, offer them a partly digested fly so that they can feed more easily. The female Eresid spider *Stegodyphus lineatus* pays the ultimate price of motherhood. After guarding the eggs, she effectively commits suicide by allowing the brood to kill her and consume her body. As most female spiders only breed once, they might just as well give their offspring a good start in life by donating the nutrients left in their flesh. In spiders, it is more usual for the males to be cannibalized by their larger mates during or after copulation.

In dung beetles, the male's dilemma is a simple one: if he does not provide a store of food for his mate and their joint offspring, his procreative activity will come to nothing. The sexes therefore exploit each other to a remarkable degree to ensure that they raise some offspring. In these fascinating creatures, the high level of parental co-operation has evolved because of the scattered and ephemeral nature of the food which they and their grubs consume. When the nutritious commodity splatters on to the ground, there is a race to win a share of it, not only from various kinds of beetles but also from flies, fungi and other coprophagous organisms. In the Serengeti National Park in Tanzania, a fresh heap of elephant droppings is hot property and can attract dung beetles at the rate of 4000 an hour. The first individuals on the scene are therefore under extreme pressure to collect and hide as much of the stuff as possible, for their own use as well as for their larvae.

Although the detailed behaviour varies from species to species, in essence, by operating as a team, a male and female can shift and bury more dung more quickly than one beetle slaving away on its own. Furthermore, in those species which carry dung away, beetles can still have their valuable cargo hijacked by rivals. So while the male stands on his head and uses his back legs to propel the sphere of excrement

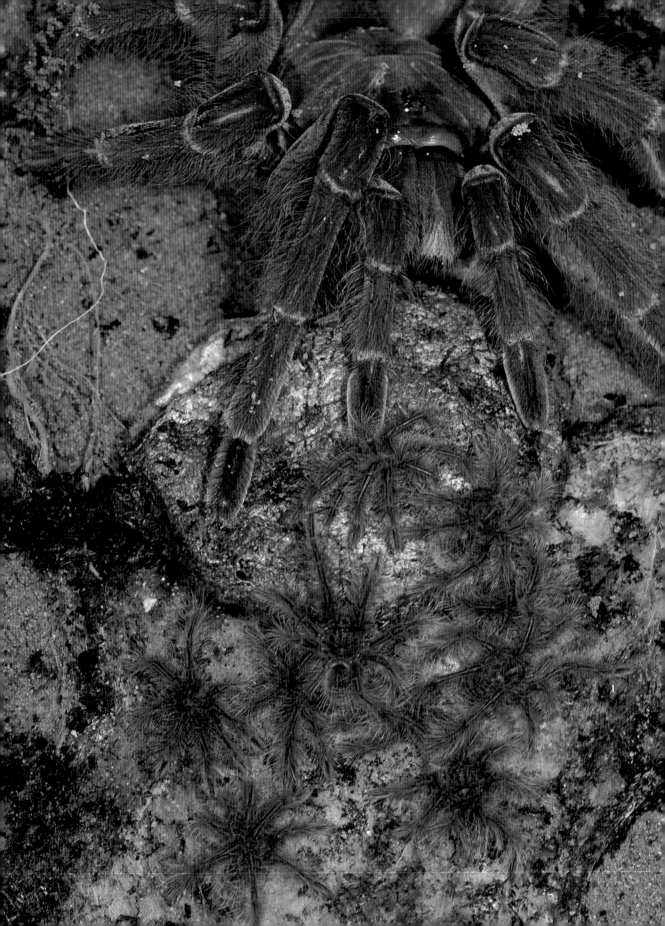

backwards, the female 'rides shotgun' on top to fend off would-be robbers. Should the ball meet a snag, the female helps her partner to set it rolling again before resuming her lofty position. When they have reached a safe distance away from the pat, the male puts his back into the job of burying the dung, along with the female, which still clings to the top of it. The interred bolus forms the basis of a food store for both the larvae and the female. Although the couple may already have mated, they generally copulate during the final stages of the burial – thus ensuring that the male is genuinely the father of the ·grubs for which he has laboured so hard.

Once the nest is completed, the male tends not to linger, but breaks out to woo and roll dung with another female. Meanwhile, his original mate stays underground and reworks the store of dung in preparation for the eggs. This can take nearly two weeks. Once the eggs are hatched, her task is not over, because she spends her time keeping moulds, fungi, termites and ants at bay. In all, a female dung beetle may devote nearly two months to rearing between one and four offspring, during which period she will devour over half the dung herself. This might seem rather a poor return on such a large investment of time, and yet unguarded nests are invariably overwhelmed by other dung-consumers and the eggs and larvae do not survive.

LEFT The long wait is over: a female tarantula is rewarded for her lone vigil. For two weeks she starved while guarding her eggs. These spiderlings will carry on her genes.

RIGHT A tasty takeaway. Both male and female scarab beetles are forced to co-operate if they are to provide sufficient nourishing dung for their joint brood.

Birds – a diversity of strategies

Although few species take parental care to the extremes adopted by the wandering albatross, it is not difficult to fathom why advanced levels of guardianship should be a hallmark of birds. They are supercharged creatures, extremely active and hot-blooded, with young which hatch either in a fairly helpless state and/or much smaller than their parents. For many species, the chicks are under enormous pressure to grow so that they can reach sexual maturity as quickly as possible – usually within a year. To enable this to happen, their little bodies must be crammed with a never-ending supply of highly nutritious food. For the majority of birds, their energetic lifestyle has trapped them into serious parenting, binding the sexes not only to each other but also to their young offspring.

There is a fascinating aspect to avian parenting. Birds perhaps more than any other group of animals show how the environment plays a key role in driving the separate interests of males and females. This in turn influences the nature of their parental strategies. For instance, we have become accustomed to the fact that it is usually females which are curbed in their reproductive potential by the number of eggs they are able to produce. But in some birds, the hens have access to such rich supplies of food that they can produce clutch after clutch without a break. This state of affairs turns the tables on maverick males by encouraging the females to take multiple sexual partners. But as each clutch must be incubated when it is completed, the hens have to recruit the cocks to act as egg-sitters and chick-minders. What now constrains the females is the availability of free males for whom they may have to fight.

A bird which practises this kind of polyandry is the jacana. Jacanas inhabit tropical pools and lakes and can pick their way across floating vegetation, spreading their weight on their very long toes – hence their alternative name of 'lily-trotters'. Bearing a vermilion shield on their foreheads, American jacanas have reddish-brown plumage with brilliant golden-green pinions which are conspicuous in flight. But it is their breeding arrangements that make these birds especially interesting: the females practise a particularly extreme form of polyandry, with the males undertaking all the duties normally performed by their partners.

A female jacana enjoys the services of several males, which do all the work of building the floating nests, incubating the eggs for nearly a month until they hatch and then caring for the chicks for a further two months. They make devoted fathers and when danger threatens any of the brood, the chicks either shelter beneath his wings or, on a call from him, sink under the water with only the tip of their bill showing so that they can breathe. The females are 75 per cent larger than their mates, do all the courting and scrap among themselves for territories. The most successful fighters are the heaviest with the biggest, reddest wattles. The shields display a record of their owner's fighting history, as the scars of old injuries are yellow. Such fierce females may manage to defend a territory with as many as six males. Within her area, each male has his own nest located in his own patch of vegetation, but as he is relatively puny, he is unable to drive off trespassing females. When there is a female intruder, he screams for his own mate to defend his share of her freehold. In the event of a new hen taking over, the males make a feeble attempt to expel her, but within a few hours they have accepted the inevitable and mate with her. Such takeovers are bad news for the vanquished females, because the victor will set about destroying the eggs and methodically hunting down the chicks of her predecessor so that she can immediately employ the males to look after her own eggs.

In effect, a female jacana acts like a fierce egg factory with no constraint on her production line, completing a clutch of four every ten days or so. By contrast, the reproductive potential of each of her partners is severely limited because, once he has received a clutch of eggs, the male is tied up with parental responsibilities for the best part of three months. The female's sexual potential is limited only by the number of males she can exploit and retain in the face of serious competition from other hens.

Apart from laying eggs, hen jacanas behave just like the strutting cocks of other species – they are big, aggressive, passionate and less choosy than most females about their sexual partners. On the other hand, their mates act like traditional hens – the caring, gentler sex. This is such a reversal of the normal situation that it raises the question, what are the special circumstances which favour the evolution of polyandry on such a scale?

The answer may be found in the rich environment which jacanas inhabit. With no shortage of moisture and heated by the tropical sun, the swamps are among the most productive places on the planet. Such is their immense fertility that it has been estimated that the calorific value of the food available in 1 square metre (10 square feet) of ground is equivalent to two dozen chocolate bars. In fact, for the jacanas, these places are like open bird tables groaning with goodies. So easy are the pickings that, unlike most female birds, hen jacanas have evolved into 'battery hens', churning out egg after egg with little physiological stress. They have therefore seized the reproductive initiative, pursuing a strategy of continuous egg production while coercing a coterie of males into incubating the eggs and guarding the chicks.

Hen pecked: a male pheasant-tailed jacana from Sri Lanka and his new chick. Like his American cousins, he may be one of many males completely under the control of a dominant female, and he does all the parenting.

Unfortunately, there are never enough males to satisfy the lusty hens, so they are the ones which have been forced into fighting for mates, in the same way that males of most other bird species compete for their partners. Accordingly, large, aggressive hen jacanas win larger harems of males. The only thing the hens cannot do is shunt the cost of egg production on to their partners – only the females of the species have the anatomical equipment to manufacture well-provisioned eggs.

Jacanas are not the only birds to indulge in polyandry. Several kinds of shore birds practise it on their Arctic or sub-Arctic breeding grounds. Although the windy and bitterly cold winters maintain the tundra as an environment of bonsai plants, during the eternal days of midsummer there is an explosion of life – especially of insects – which many millions of migrant birds exploit for raising their families. Because of the brief bonanza of food, the females are able to make many eggs during a short period. This is a scenario that favours emancipated females and male mothers. In the three kinds of phalarope – wading birds which spend much of the winter offshore – the hens are the more colourful sex and court their duller partners, which take over the first clutch of eggs.

This leaves the females free to lay at least one more clutch, which might be fathered either by her initial mate or by another partner. Sometimes she incubates the second or third clutch and so increases the number of her progeny. In phalaropes and other shore birds such as Temminck's stints and sanderling, the chicks hatch in a relatively advanced state, having undergone more of their development inside the eggs. Consequently, the eggs of such 'precocial' species are relatively large – in the spotted sandpiper, a clutch of four is equivalent to 80 per cent of the hen's body weight. Such massive eggs drain the female's resources. It therefore pays the male sandpiper to take over the clutch as soon as it is completed, which enables his mate to fatten up and perhaps produce another brood, thereby realizing her maximum reproductive potential in the short northern summer. But from the cock's point of view there is a down side to this generosity. Once he has assumed full responsibility for the eggs, the hen is free to mate with whom she chooses. In many cases, she probably opts for a change of sexual partner to receive her second and third batches of eggs.

Single mothers

Examples of polyandry are few and far between for the simple reason that the environment rarely gives females such an easy ride as it does the jacanas and Arctic wading birds. For most birds, finding enough extra food to manufacture eggs packed with nutrients is an arduous business. World wide, hen birds are constrained in the number of eggs they can lay in a season and so they, as the limited resource, are fought over by the males – which are then free to copulate with as many partners as they can secure. In most wading birds, wildfowl and members of the pheasant and grouse family, all parental duties are shifted firmly on to the females. Their mates play no part in incubation or protecting their vulnerable chicks after they have emerged from the eggs.

In all of these cases, the young are hatched in a relatively advanced state and can run around and forage for themselves. The parent which defects – whether it is the cock in the polygamous birds or the hen in the polyandrous species – is therefore not needed as a provider of food, which makes his or her desertion that much easier.

But there can be intense rivalry betweem single mothers and lone fathers. Barrow's golden eye, for example, is a tough little diving duck and one population breeds on Lake Myvatn in Iceland. The females nest alongside fast flowing rivers leading out of the lake, and when the ducklings hatch the mother leads them on a perilous journey upstream to the best feeding areas. The journey is dangerous because they literally risk their lives getting there.

If they pass a male whose female is late hatching and still sitting on eggs, he mercilessly beats them to death, because he doesn't want any ducklings competing with his own offspring. If they survive that hurdle and reach the feeding area, other females already there will also attack and kill newcomers to protect the best sources of food for their own broods. In July each year, the upper reaches of Lake Myvatn can be a scene of carnage, with hundreds of dead ducklings – the result of mothers ferociously fighting for the interests of their own broods at the expense of others.

Parents pulling together?

The majority of birds probably live in environments which are middling – meaning that there is generally a glut of food during the nesting season which is sufficient to enable single parents to rear families, but if both parents join forces they can between them rear larger ones. As an alternative, the environment may also be able to support one or other of the parents helping to rear two broods simultaneously. It is in these circumstances, where the role of parenting has not been placed firmly on to one or other of the sexes, that all options have been subject to negotiation. Even the evolution of chicks which hatch helpless, blind and naked might have been a female tactic in the battle of the sexes. After all, such underdeveloped young generally hatch from relatively small and poorly provisioned eggs and so vastly reduce the female's initial investment in reproduction, forcing their mates to share some of the burden of 'growing them'.

For the average songbird of the woods and hedgerows, parenting is a tug of war in which the number of young, the number of broods and who rears them have been settled. Little of this battle is obvious on the surface. After all, small birds such as finches and the various kinds of tits – like the great tit – seem to display impressive industry and parental co-operation during the spring and summer. As great tits rarely live for more than one year, they are under immense pressure to continue their lines. Nesting against the clock, they time their attempts to raise their families to coincide with seasonal gluts of food. The hen needs to deliver her eggs so that by the time they hatch caterpillars are abundant. To stand a chance of fledging within three weeks, the nestlings must increase their weight by fifteen-fold – a human baby takes over ten years to achieve that amount of growth. Whether the young birds succeed depends almost entirely on the foraging skills and dedication of their parents. Hunting in the well-stocked canopy within their territory, the mother and father make up to 600 visits a day to the nest, each time carrying a succulent caterpillar or a nourishing insect. This adds up to an incredible 10,000 morsels of food delivered to the family before the youngsters are ready to fly.

And yet we know that each sex still has its own agenda to pursue, with both partners attempting to make the relationship work in their favour. Sophisticated DNA 'fingerprinting' has revealed damning evidence that chicks within single nests are often of mixed parentage, showing that both sexes frequently engage in sneaky affairs. Given the opportunity, the cocks try to father a few extra chicks on the side, while maintaining their initial partners on the home front. They in turn may well be cuckolded; half of all swallow nests have eggs fertilized by more than one male, while in Australia every nest of the blue fairy wren shows evidence of rampant avian promiscuity. Infidelity may be a ploy used by the hens as a means of improving the genetic constitution of their offspring. Male pied flycatchers even set up mistresses.

At first sight, the cock pied flycatcher does not look like the kind of bird that specializes in sexual deception, and yet the males are confirmed bigamists. They are somewhat pot-bellied, short-tailed birds, rather smaller than sparrows, and they breed in forested areas from the Atlantic seaboard of Europe right the way across Russia to Siberia. After spending the winter in West Africa, they arrive in their breeding grounds in spring – the cocks a week ahead of the hens in order to establish their territories and select their nest holes. These have usually been drilled out by woodpeckers or are cavities which have arisen where branches have broken away from the trunks. However, pied flycatchers take very readily to nest boxes, and in many woodlands and sylvan gardens the number of breeding pairs of these delightful birds has been boosted by the provision of artificial nesting sites.

Once a cock is settled in his territory, he sings incessantly to attract a hen. When one shows interest, he tries to impress her with his display flights and leads her to the nest site, perching in the entrance while flicking his wings and fanning his tail. If, on inspecting the chamber, she likes what she sees and the surrounding vegetation promises to yield enough caterpillars during the summer to feed her family, she consents to copulate with the male. When the weather warms and the leaf buds burst, she lays her light blue eggs, one each morning, until the clutch of six or seven is completed. The appearance of the last egg marks the start of a two-week period of incubation which is carried out solely by the hen. Even before the clutch was completed her partner left to pursue other interests!

Having established one hen in a prime nesting site, the cock flits off to find another breeding hole – but not too close to his original 'home'. On average, he will try and set up a second territory 200 metres (220 yards) or so away from his first mate, although some individuals may fly several kilometres before settling down to advertise for a second female. Putting some distance between the territories might

ABOVE The philanderer. The male pied flycatcher (left) is a bigamist, conning two females to father his chicks, but only one gets his full attention as a parent.

ABOVE RIGHT Who dares wins. A battle of nerves is waged between male and female penduline tits. Too slow off the mark means getting left with the babies.

OPPOSITE Happy family? Male and female bullfinches share nest duties. When the sexes co-operate in this way, it is generally in their own selfish reproductive interests. They rear more offspring carrying their own genes.

be part of the cock's deception – unattached hens might not realize that he is already paired. Not all males are successful bigamists, but for one in every four or five philandering pays off and he pairs up again. However, the second 'wife' does not get the male's undivided attention; once she is sitting on a full complement of eggs, the male is tugged back to his first mate by the demands of his original family. As the nestlings are about to hatch, he gives them priority, deserting his 'mistress' in the most caddish way.

Although the original hen loses little from her mate's dalliance because she gains his full-time assistance when looking after the brood, the deceived female is hard pressed as a single mother to keep her nestlings alive and may manage to rear only about half of them. The cock pied flycatcher wins all round because, through his bigamy, he manages to father a few extra chicks.

However, there is at least one species in which the hens hit back! As their name suggests, penduline tits are small tit-like birds which inhabit Eurasian wetlands. They look like little avian bandits with a reddish back and a pale head masked by long black eye-patches. The birds often breed around willow-fringed lakes, marshes and rivers where their pouched nests, skilfully constructed from bulrush down, dangle from twigs, often over water. Although they appear to be flimsy and precariously placed, the nests are strongly woven to their supports. The fluff from which they are largely made assists the females to deceive their mates.

The cock starts to construct the nest – indeed, he may begin to build several before attracting a partner. Once the pouch is nearly finished, the couple mate frequently in the branches above the nest. With the arrival of the eggs, the scene is set for a real conflict as both sexes attempt to get the best deal without jeopardizing their offspring.

As each of these tiny birds is capable of bringing up a batch of nestlings single-handed, both of them attempt to foist the task on to the other. Which one is landed with the role of parent is a matter of timing. Although the cock is the dominant partner during the early stages of courtship, the hen becomes increasingly aggressive towards him as she approaches the egg-laying period. When about to lay, she disappears inside the cramped nest chamber and is reluctant for her partner to enter until she has, in a frenzy of activity, covered her egg in fluff. Each day, her pattern of behaviour is similar – she copulates with the male and every additional egg is buried in the floor of the nest before her mate is allowed to come in. It is a tricky situation, because if he discovers her secret hoard he is likely to abandon the nest, forcing her to stay and care for the family, while he sets up home with another hen. But if the hen's ploy works and she manages to deceive her mate, she will reveal the full clutch only after laying the last egg. Early in the morning she smartly elopes, leaving the cock to become a single parent, while she recuperates and forms another sexual relationship with a new partner.

The dilemma in which the birds find themselves is plain to see. Neither partner wishes to lose the clutch, but if they can fob the responsibility for it on to the other without jeopardizing the brood, so much the better. So, as soon as the cock sees evidence that his partner has produced eggs, it pays him to find more females with whom to mate. The same consideration holds true for the female – once she has laid one lot of eggs, it is in her reproductive interest to produce another clutch, provided she can con her first partner into staying home. In many cases, she manages to do so!

Backyard battles The observations of birds battling to achieve arrangements for the care of their offspring are gathered in scientific journals and classified as 'mating systems', of which monogamy and polygamy are the most common. But there are others. Polygynandry is practised by tundra-breeding Lapland buntings, in which the hens have several males and the cock birds possess multiple mates. But there is one demure little bird which exploits every possible system – the dunnock or hedge sparrow. It elegantly shows that whether it be monogamy, polyandry or polygynandry, the parental arrangement is nothing more than a hard fought-over compromise between cocks and hens.

Dunnocks breed in shrubs and bushes in many European parks and gardens, and their humble appearance conceals the fact that they are at odds with their opposite numbers to obtain the best deal out of sex. Males try and father the maximum number of chicks with as many females as possible, and every female would like to reduce the effort of parenting by enlisting the help of several males to rear her family. There is no perfect resolution, and the arrangement that each individual chips out for itself tends to reflect its quality. A dominant cock persuades a pair of hens to breed with him – very much to his reproductive benefit, although each hen fares worse in individual productivity. A highly desirable hen wins the gender battle when she manages to enslave two males to rear her chicks. When neither sex can acquire a second partner, uneasy monogamy prevails – at least the male is reasonably sure of his paternity, albeit with a reduced number of offspring, and the hen, with her mate's help, raises more chicks than she would in a polygamous relationship. Polygynandry – with two cocks and two hens – can be regarded as a 'stalemate' in the sexual conflict; the top male cannot evict the second one and so has to share the hens, and the dominant hen cannot drive out the other, nor claim both males exclusively for herself. This 'backyard battle' is a reminder that monogamy is just as much an uneasy alliance as relationships involving multiple husbands and wives.

Mammals: natural-born mothers

In just over 90 per cent of birds, monogamy prevails. This reflects the near impossibility of females producing an unlimited supply of eggs in most habitats, and the fact that male birds are able to make a significant contribution to the survival of the chicks. But there is one major group of creatures in which this is not so – the mammals. Among these equally hot-blooded, very active animals, monogamy is confined to a mere 5 per cent; in the rest the males have completely opted out of parenting. There are special reasons why female mammals are natural-born single mothers.

Mammals are blessed with bodies which can be regarded as the pinnacle of design for coping with unpredictable conditions. Covered with insulating fur or a layer of fat, they have developed an advanced system of temperature control which has enabled them to colonize some of the hottest and coldest places on Earth. In pressing themselves into almost every corner of the planet, mammals have evolved a stupendous range of shapes and sizes – from the smallest shrew, bat or rodent barely half the length of a human thumb to the gigantic blue whale. Without a doubt, milk is a major key to mammalian success, and this exceptional form of infant food is produced solely by mother mammals; it can be stored and delivered at will to their offspring in places which are secure from enemies.

But for female mammals, the ability to function as milk bars is both liberating and stressful. Pregnancy gives them a measure of freedom by allowing them to carry their developing offspring in their wombs while they search for extra food – a human female,  for instance, needs to divert 80,000 calories of nourishment over the course of her pregnancy to 'grow' her new baby. Surplus food is converted into reserves of fat, and ultimately milk. However, female mammals' unique abilities have turned them into self-contained single parents. With internal fertilization, pregnancy and a set of glands that supply baby food on demand, they have effectively uncoupled their mates from the parental process. The males are thus free to cheat, competing among themselves to sire as many offspring as possible through sexual philandering. This scenario encourages the evolution of brawling, polgynous males and very finicky females. Whereas every mature female gets to breed, many males never have an opportunity to mate – in grey seals, only one in ten bulls father any offspring and those that do, take no interest them.

There are exceptions. In mammals, the choice of breeding system is largely determined by the male and depends upon how he can best produce the most offspring. In well over half the species, the females live alone and the males defend a territory which embraces the home ranges of several females – like many solitary carnivores such as foxes or leopards. By inseminating a number of females, the males take the chance that a few of their offspring may survive, despite the fact that they invest no effort in their upbringing. An alternative tactic is for the male to stay with one female and help her to raise their joint family. But such a male returns to the parental fold for purely selfish reasons – by striking up a co-operative relationship with the females with whom he has mated, he increases the likelihood of their offspring surviving.

Baby-sitting fathers

Monogamous relationships are strewn thinly across the mammals. Although, from the human perspective, they appear to resemble caring and sharing partnerships, they are generally lifestyles which are forced upon a few species by some aspect of the environment. There is often little that the males can do in terms of caring for their young. Indeed, they may forcibly eject them from their range when the offspring grow up.

Dwarf antelopes – such as the klipspringers and dik-diks of southern and eastern Africa – are unusual among hoofed animals in that they go around in pairs.

OPPOSITE Food on the hoof. In most mammals the female provides the sole care for the offspring, including a ready supply of nourishing milk.

RIGHT Devoted couples. The dik-dik is unusual for mammals in that the males and females stick to each other like glue. If they didn't they could lose each other in the cluttered under-growth and the male might jeopardize his paternity.

They frequent cluttered bush and thickly vegetated forest habitats where nourishing herbage of the kind that they like is widely scattered. It therefore pays these animals to be territorial so that they can acquire an intimate knowledge of the places where their food occurs. The buck, which is often slightly smaller than his mate, ensures success in the paternity stakes by commandeering an area of desirable bush and then behaving as a constant consort to his female, never moving more than a few paces from her side for fear of losing sight of her in the dense vegetation – and possibly losing his sexual monopoly of her as well. It has been recorded that a pair of klipspringers spend their entire adult lives literally within 5 metres (16 feet) of each other. When the fawns arrive, the female cares for them, though the father is always nearby, preoccupied with guarding the mother.

Such lifelong bonds lessen the competition between males and so preclude the need for large, aggressive bucks of the kind found in deer and some larger antelope. There is an interesting comparison to be made with the Ugandan kob, in which the males reduce the difficulty of locating females which forage over very large expanses of countryside by advertising for them in arenas (see Chapter 2).

A similar situation prevails in gibbons. These singing apes from South-East Asia appear to live like happily married couples together with their immature children. However, on close inspection, it can be seen that a male gibbon is not so much a caring father as the guardian of the adult female with whom he has chosen to breed. He is also a valiant defender of the swathe of jungle through which she and their joint offspring need to forage for tender leaves and ripe fruit. For a male gibbon, monogamy pays reproductive dividends; by keeping a close track of his 'wife' in the complex, cluttered canopy of the rain-forest, he can be sure of fathering her offspring. Uniquely among apes, male gibbons are virtually indistinguishable from their mates – a characteristic that reflects the low level of competition for females. Only the male siamang – the largest of the gibbons, from the Malay Peninsula and Sumatra – shows a high level of paternal interest, taking over the daily care of his infant when it is about a year old and continuing to look after it closely for the next two years.

The advantage of the direct involvement of the male has been measured for the aardwolf, a very unusual member of the hyena family. Although its body has the unmistakable sloping appearance of the more familiar spotted hyena, its muzzle is far more delicate, befitting an animal which lives on insects. Equipped with much reduced dentition and a long, mobile tongue covered with glutinous saliva, these shy animals emerge under the cover of darkness to feed on a few kinds of snouted harvester termites. Unlike clan-living spotted hyenas, aardwolves live in widely scattered pairs which lay claim to their large foraging territories by scent-marking and by vigorously attacking intruders. They search for termite mounds by themselves and even sleep in separate dens.

When it comes to breeding, a dominant male aardwolf has the best of both worlds. He copulates with his own partner, mating with her for over four hours to ensure his paternity. He then keeps a very close eye on her to make sure that no other male slips in for a little sneaky sex. Once the danger is over, he becomes sneaky himself and moves around the territories of lower-status males to see if any of their females are willing to mate with him. In his quest for extra-curricular sex, he may well be successful, but he does not abandon his original partner – and for good reason.

The problem that any mother aardwolf faces is that in order to get sufficient nourishment to maintain lactation, she needs to consume a nightly ration of a quarter of a million termites – a formidable task that will take her away from the den for perhaps eight hours. When the pups are small and confined inside the den, the mother can safely leave them while she forages, but later on, when they start to explore outside, the situation changes. During this period, her offspring are likely to attract predators, among whom spotted hyenas rank as the most serious cub-killers. This is precisely when the male aardwolf starts to take an interest in his family. So, every evening before the mother departs, the male turns up at the den and dutifully watches over the site while his young charges play rough-and-tumble games. If anything threatens them, he will chase it away. Furthermore, he will not leave until the female returns and disappears inside the den to suckle the young.

The male's vigil is very much in his interest because a pair of aardwolves manages to rear between one and two cubs a year (the average is 1.5 on the South African veldt), whereas a single mother without the benefit of a male baby-sitter is lucky to raise any cubs at all (the average for a lone mother aardwolf is 0.3 cubs a year). By pursuing a monogamous relationship and guarding the cubs when they are at their most vulnerable, a male aardwolf improves his reproductive success fivefold. Put another way, he would have to sire the litters of at least six single females to better the results of his baby-sitting arrangements with one partner!

Several members of the dog family – including wolves, jackals, bat-eared foxes and African wild dogs – form bonds between the sexes, and the males make a valuable contribution to rearing the offspring. Such parental involvement undoubtedly helps to sustain their predatory way of life and breeding productivity. Firstly, the pack species live extravagantly, creaming off large and hugely nutritious prey such as wildebeest and caribou at the top of the food chains. They are able to achieve this only by hunting in groups, and in this males and females play an equal role. Secondly, the quarry has to be searched for over large areas, often far away from where the pups may be housed, and so food must be transported back to the den. Although the males cannot suckle, they pull their weight by regurgitating half-digested meat to the pups.

Most intriguing of all mammalian fathers may turn out to be the Dayak fruit bats. Male bats typically have nothing to do with the youngsters which they father, but a few male Dayak fruit bats caught in the Krau Game Reserve in Malaysia showed evidence of lactation. They were perfectly healthy specimens, with large testes actively producing sperm, and yet small amounts of milk were expressed from their well-formed mammary glands. Although the small size of their nipples indicated that they had not been suckled, the discovery does raise the possibility that some of the males of this species might be milking fathers.

Males of the saddle-backed tamarin also act as baby-sitters. Found in Peru, they are one of the smallest of the primates, with a squirrel-like lifestyle. However, each mature female lives harmoniously with two males which can mate with her at any

ABOVE A caring father.
The male African wild dog
does his bit for the offspring
by regurgitating a meal of
partially digested meat
for a hungry pup.

LEFT Family love.
In primates like these
mountain gorillas the bond
between mother and off-
spring is essential to rear a
slow-growing, helpless baby.
The warrior father guards
the troop and its territory.

time, even when she is pregnant and suckling. This co-operative polyandry might have evolved because the females give birth to twins which, being both tiny and vulnerable, need constant attention and protection. As the mother has to feed intensively, she uses the two males to carry the babies. It is in their interest to assist her; otherwise they might have nothing to show for their sexual activity. But why should these males help each other rather than compete for the female's favours? By allowing them complete sexual access, and by concealing the signs of her ovulation, the female keeps the males in the dark as to which one of them is the real father. So rather than risk abandoning their own babies, the males become committed parents. However, such caring fathers are rare among mammals – most have evolved as warrior guardians.

Guardian males

Primates are among the most social of mammals. Although the sexes live in cohesive groups (see Chapter 5), the males are rarely involved in parental duties. Indeed, in these animals, the difference between the sexes is exacerbated by the fact that males have become specialized guardians, good at getting what they want by force if necessary, whereas females excel as dedicated mothers. Take mountain gorillas, for instance.

The largest of the great apes, a few hundred of these shaggy-coated creatures roam the dank cloud forests which clothe the mountains on the borders of Rwanda, Uganda and the Congo People's Republic (formerly Zaire). They live in 'families' of varying size, but an average one might consist of three or four adult females, five or so youngsters of widely differing ages and one fully mature male. Called a silverback because of his very pale grey 'saddle', the adult male is an awesome creature, twice the weight of any member of his harem, with massive shoulders, a high domed head accommodating powerful jaw muscles, and canine teeth to match. As if to reinforce his image of unmitigated ferocity, his visage is framed by a beard and thatch of long black hair. Everything about the silverback communicates a single message loud and clear – he is not to be meddled with. Should there be any doubt about his potential as a fighter, his threat display when he is angered is enough to freeze the blood. Roaring in fury, he charges on all fours, slapping the ground and perhaps snapping off a sapling or two. As he closes in on the animal which has provoked him, he rises on his hind legs and with his cupped hands beats a tattoo on his chest. If sufficiently aroused, he will follow through with a merciless attack, putting his fangs to good use and pounding his opponent with his dinner-plate sized hands.

The silverback gorilla is both warrior and guardian – the outcome of an evolutionary trend which started with his less impressive ancestors competing for sex.

Then as now, females constituted a resource for reproduction; the bigger and fiercer the males were, the more females they gathered around them and the greater the number of offspring they left. Males needed to be large and violent in order to compete among themselves for females, and to be able to retain them. In the case of mountain gorillas, the females are not especially seasonal in coming into oestrus (which they do only once in every three to five years) and so the male's best chance of breeding is to accompany them so as to catch each and every one of them when they become sexually receptive. But there is also another advantage in cohabiting. The females look to their silverback for protection both for themselves and for their offspring. Certainly, the male will defend any of his group – including his youngsters – without hesitation should any of them be attacked, though this is as far as his direct parental involvement will go. But there is more. In order to fulfil their roles as mothers, the females need the powerful presence of the silverback to protect a resource that they require in plenty – food.

There is evidence that diet has a profound effect on female fertility in primates. Better nourished ones begin to breed at an earlier age, produce healthier young, have shorter intervals between pregnancies and live longer. So, while males might improve their breeding chances by fighting over sexually receptive females, females can improve theirs by access to high-quality foods that will improve their condition. In mountain gorillas, the males assist their mates to feed as best they can. These great apes are vegetarian, browsing chiefly on foliage and the stalks of wild celery. The ground beneath the moss-wreathed canopy is covered with the stuff, but gorillas need huge amounts of it, especially the nursing mothers. They rarely clear an area of their favourite plants, but they must allow time for the foliage to regenerate after they have fed, so the groups are always on the move. This brings them into potential conflict with neighbours. Although mountain gorillas are not strictly territorial, each group moves around a home area which overlaps those of other families and the male will, if necessary, fight to exclude outsiders from his favoured part of the forest. Despite his indifference as a hands-on father, the silverback mountain gorilla is a supreme minder, maintaining a kind of 'cold war' peace in which all his 'family' can thrive.

Once the parents have different roles to play, inevitably the sexes will be driven apart in the sense that males will tend towards becoming bigger and more pugnacious because they will produce more offspring that way, while females will become more protective and dedicated as mothers. The problem faced by many social animals is how to prevent tensions caused by highly sexed, competitive and aggressive males from tearing the groups apart.

CHAPTER

5

FAMILY
AFFAIRS

Sex is divisive, disruptive and often destructive. The urge to reproduce frequently manifests itself in aggression, shattering social groups and driving animals to lead independent lives. Males are especially violent, battling over territories, jealously fighting for what they regard as their own and making as many sexual conquests as possible. Because the biggest or perhaps the most beautiful bullies have preferential access to females, a lot of unsuccessful and frustrated males are left seething on the sidelines. Females, too, are capable of spinning their own webs of intrigue. As each mother is rooting only for her own offspring, she may attempt to spoil a rival female's chances of breeding, or even surreptitiously maltreat or murder another mother's infants to enhance the prospects of her own. Such activities are hardly conducive to smoothly running societies.

PREVIOUS PAGES
Neighbourhood watch:
a family of meerkats on
the look out. By protecting
each other, an individual
makes sure some relatives,
carrying some of its own
genes, survive.

And yet a whole range of creatures manage to live in communities of one kind or another. The question arises as to how sex as a major source of tension is kept under control in species which, perhaps for environmental reasons, need to live in highly organized communities? What behavioural conventions enable hot-tempered males hyped up on testosterone to co-exist? How do females cope with males behaving badly and avoid being raped? These are difficulties which can never be fully resolved, because the battle of the sexes is fundamentally a process of continuing evolutionary negotiation between parties with quite different interests. The lifestyle of the gelada baboon illustrates how the uneasy relationship between oppressive males and fearful females works out in this very sociable primate.

A male gelada in his prime looks every inch a despot. His long, chiselled face with eyes framed deeply by a heavy, aggressive brow is surrounded by a wild cascade of buff-brown hair, and from his shoulders flows a thick cape of long fur which makes him look a lot larger than he really is. Alert to everything that is going on around him, he commands with almost absolute authority a family of six or seven smaller and skinnier wives and their offspring. In the dramatic highlands of Ethiopia, where these ground-feeding monkeys occur, the male needs to be vigilant because he lives in a troop several hundred strong alongside other overlords and gangs of sex-starved bachelors which are constantly threatening to take his precious wives from him. His body signals combined with his irascible nature are his defence. His chief form of deterrence is his savage stare, made all the more startling by a rapid flash of his eyebrows, which stand out white against his charcoal-black face. If this is not sufficient to generate a frisson of fear in those which risk his wrath, he makes his visage even more intimidating by flipping his upper lip backwards over his nostrils to reveal a great expanse of pink gum and the ultimate weapons underpinning his authority – a pair of murderous canine teeth which would do justice to any carnivore. Such threats are usually sufficient to thwart any argument. However, if the source of irritation continues, the male explodes in fury: barking like a dog and grimacing madly, he charges through the troop with his cape flailing from side to side, scattering all before him until he intercepts the baboon which has displeased him. Screaming with fear, the offending animal is given a good slapping and perhaps a bite that it will remember for some time.

No member of the troop is immune from the male's temper. His most violent attacks are likely to be saved for the confident young bachelors which dare to challenge him for his harem, but even his 'wives' are wary of his anger and may be beaten without mercy, especially if they refuse to submit when he tries to force them into copulating.

However, even despots get their come-uppance in the end. Although individually the females are no match for the male's superior muscle power, they can stand together. The dominant males always want their own way and, when hungry, they bully their wives into moving away from food before they have taken their fill. However, occasionally the wives gang up, screaming defiantly in unison, and cause their husband to back off.

Of course, the mother of all fights for the despot is his final show-down when, after perhaps two years in power, he is toppled by whichever of the bachelors feels confident and strong enough to mount a challenge for the females. Although the original male will probably have lost some of his fitness, he will defend his position to the best of his ability, causing mayhem as he and his opponent charge through the troop, snarling and lashing out at each other. In the end, the old male may be injured and step down. Curiously, the broken tyrant often lurks around on the periphery of his former family, where he is tolerated for a short time by the male which usurped him. The takeover generally heralds a period of instability for the harem. The victorious male is inevitably inexperienced at disciplining a group of females, so they tend to wander apart and become prey to the attentions of other overlords and feisty bachelors.

Despite all the violence and apparent chaos in gelada groups, these animals still live together in troops up to 600 strong – bigger than the societies of any other primate, barring our own. So why do animals live in such super-families if this means exposing themselves to daily lives fraught with tension?

Milling masses

Many species which live in groups are not social in the full meaning of the word. A pinnacle of granite covered with tens of thousands of nesting gannets may look like a smoothly running sea-bird city, yet it is very much a community of strangers with an armed tolerance of each other. Like all sea-birds, gannets must return to the land to breed, and they settle in colonies in traditional locations. Each pair defends with great vigour a meagre territory on which its nest is positioned just beyond stabbing distance of the hostile neighbours. Gannets, in common with the majority of colonial birds, exhibit virtually nothing in the way of co-ordinated social behaviour. However, the bickering couples may benefit from being close to each other, because the chosen cliffs and islands are free from terrestrial thieves such as foxes. Furthermore, with the presence of so many courting couples, the colonies may act as highly erotic theatres, enhancing the level of sexual excitement, which assists synchronous nesting.

Bad neighbours forced to tolerate each other: quarrelsome gannets derive great benefits from breeding together on crowded cliffs.

This itself may be an important anti-predator ploy, swamping the market for a limited period with so many eggs and chicks that the gannet's avian enemies – such as greater black-backed gulls – cannot possibly devour them all.

When there are predators about, the more eyes and ears the better. Not surprisingly, animals which feature largely on the menu of others often tend towards some degree of gregariousness. When 'birds of a feather' – like starlings or knots – flock together, they perform some of the most thrilling shows in the natural world. Larger terrestrial animals also form huge anonymous herds, especially during migration. Both wildebeest and caribou, for example, make their annual treks in this manner. In these species, there is an overwhelming value in living together. The appearance of a peregrine falcon causes starlings and knots to close ranks immediately, presenting the enemy with a tightly bunched flock into which it would be difficult, or even suicidal, to swoop.

Too close for comfort, but essential for protection: for this herd of wildebeest on migration there is safety in numbers. A lone individual would certainly fall to predators.

By hiding among countless thousands of its fellows, an individual bird, insect or fish may be safer from predators. The only enduring relationships within these milling masses are between mothers and their young offspring.

By contrast, a properly social animal living permanently among companions is able to share in some benefit which can only be made available through the combined endeavours of a number of individuals. For instance, as we shall see later in this chapter, species of termites, ants, bees and wasps share and defend nests and, through teamwork, are able to forage more effectively and protect themselves and their broods from being eaten by much larger predators. A pack of wolves consisting of both males and females can bring a bull bison to its knees and provide food for everyone, whereas a single wolf might starve to death. Troops of primates may be able to forage efficiently in circumstances in which a lone individual would fail to survive. Fundamental to the success of social animals is that each of them must co-operate in keeping the group together, otherwise the advantages of gregariousness would vanish and so put at risk the survival of every individual. It is in these animals, where the sexes cohabit, that tensions created by so-called Machiavellian males are more of a problem.

Machiavellian males

Most observers of social species have focused their attention on the kinds of behaviour that bind animals into coherent communities, and attempted to analyse the benefits and drawbacks to the individual of being helpful, generous or even self-sacrificing towards others. They have generally concluded that the 'costs' of being altruistic are worth paying as long as they are reciprocated – a principle summed up in the saying 'I'll scratch your back if you'll scratch mine'. But little attention has been given to socially disruptive habits. Aggression, harassment and punishment are behaviours often meted out by dominant males. However, while generating unhappiness among the lower ranks, an oppressive male may be able to weld those beneath him into a disciplined group which is essential for the survival of them all.

In Renaissance Italy, the statesman and author Niccolo Machiavelli realized the virtues of oppressive rulers with no moral scruples in uniting human societies, and pondered the relative merits of being loved or feared. Love, he reasoned, is maintained by obligations which can easily be broken when it is advantageous to do so. Fear, on the other hand, never fails to command respect because of the dread of punishment. So it is with many of our closest relatives; in a number of primate species, tyrannical males constantly chastise insubordinate members of their troops and coerce reluctant females to mate with them.

Monkeys and baboons are among the cleverest and craftiest of all animals. Living in troops, they are big-brained, bright creatures, capable of playing politics, all attempting to influence those around them for their own selfish ends. Indeed, it is thought that the need for complex interactions led to the evolution of intelligence in the first place, rather than vice versa. While feeding or mutually grooming, these animals appear peaceful, but they are keenly aware of each other's rank, who is friends with whom and who must be treated with kid gloves. Such considerations create tensions that are liable to surface without much warning into bouts of bickering, or worse.

Sexuality is a major cause of strife. The ever-willing mature males are constantly exposed to the females within their troops and, when the latter come into full oestrus, the highest-ranking male – or 'clique' of males in some baboons and macaques – dictates which mates with them; this means either the top male or those which have curried favour with him. Less fortunate rivals which try to get in on the action are beaten up. This monopoly of copulation in groups where there are several mature but subordinate males is bound to lead to frustration; this in turn can explode into jealous rages in which animals may be hurt. If dominant males do not get their own way, they are likely to punish whoever they see as the culprit. Even females are frequently bullied because they are not willing to mate as often as the males would like them to – a situation which can lead to rape. In one study, almost half of all copulations in a group of wild orang-utans happened after fierce resistance by the females had been violently overcome by the males.

In many primates, sexual aggravation is rather subtle, but in hamadryas baboons – the sacred baboon revered by the ancient Egyptians – the harassment is often gratuitously handed out by males and is easy to observe. Hamadryas are swarthy animals with rather stocky legs admirably suited to scrambling around the steep gorges in the Middle East and the adjacent part of Africa where they live. The sexes are quite different from each other. Although the females look like regular brown baboons, their overlords are dressed to impress, with dog-like faces and bare buttocks in matching pink. Their dove-grey fur is fashioned in a 'poodle cut', with tufts on the head and a long cape flowing from the shoulders to the hips, making them appear as large and as formidable as possible.

These Machiavellian tyrants are dedicated polygamists, each shepherding as many as ten females to form his own personal harem, which he maintains during his prime years. Each keeps his females close by to satisfy his smouldering sexual demands. They in turn keep him company for fear of being thrashed or bitten should they wander too far from his side. Their fear is well founded, because the

ABOVE On the warpath.
A top male chimpanzee will
meet any threat to the troop
with unrestrained aggression.

LEFT Magnificent tyrant.
The dominant male gelada
baboon will not tolerate any
insubordination. His savage
stare and impressive stature
means he can rule by fear.

RIGHT Machiavellian male.
The dominant male
hamadryas baboon is a bully,
but has complete access to
all the females of his harem.
Females depend upon him
to protect them.

males are aggressive disciplinarians and frequently threaten violence by eyebrow-raising, thumping the ground, 'yawning' and whetting their upper canines against the teeth of their lower jaws. Any breach of etiquette incurs the male's wrath, often resulting in a humiliating neck bite for the offending female or a thrashing for an immature male. The females exploit the male's permanent interest in sex. They are able to vie with him for food and escape punishment simply by proffering their pink hind quarters. Presented with such an erotic appeasement gesture, the male is more likely to mount than to lash out. However, a female hamadryas which refuses to copulate with her male when he wants her to does so at her peril. Even so, many mating encounters look more like acts of aggression.

But why do females and low-ranking males stand for such oppressive treatment? As explained at the end of the last chapter, fierce males have their uses. Being born warriors, they defend the area over which the troop ranges from others which might be competing for the same food. This enables the females to devote their energies to foraging and raising their offspring. In baboons, which spend much of their time on the ground, the males are well armed with long canines and, acting in concert, scare off predators such as leopards. They may also save the females from continuous sexual harassment by unsuitable, subordinate males.

Paradoxically, despotic behaviour is fostered over the generations by the females themselves, which consistently mate with the most assertive males and pass those dominant genes on to their offspring. Nevertheless, a balance has been struck. Evil-tempered males casting a veil of fear is counter-productive if carried to extremes. Fear does not hold sway forever; the females retaliate with their own tactics. They resist being pushed around too much by forming strong friendships with each other. This might explain why they tend to spend their entire lives among their own female kin, relying on mothers, aunts, daughters and nieces to protect them from harassment. By summoning the support of a number of relatives during an argument with a high-ranking animal, an inferior individual can attain such tangible rewards as a better share of food, a more comfortable place to sleep or perhaps a more worthy mate.

The manoeuvring for better deals takes place not only *between* the sexes; females themselves are competitive and they attempt to prevent their lower-ranking companions from mating with the best males and producing pushy infants which might rival their own youngsters. An individual at the bottom of the pecking order coming into oestrus simultaneously with higher-ranking animals may be bossed around and prevented from copulating. Indeed, rough treatment may prevent her from ovulating altogether, or cause her to abort if she becomes pregnant. In these circumstances, her best chance of reproducing is to defer ovulating to a time when there is less competition for the attention of the stud male. Occasionally, cunning is called for. A subordinate female gelada baboon may take advantage of a top male when he is in a bad mood and others are avoiding him. Rather than jostling for sex with more dominant females, she waits for the male to get into a scrap. After he has finished fighting but is still stressed, she brazenly approaches him, proffers her swollen red rear and, to relieve his tension, he will sometimes mount her!

Related females and their daughters form the cores of most mammal societies and in any closely knit community there is a

Ape assignations

high risk of inbreeding. This state of affairs is not necessarily undesirable, because it conserves good genes (see Chapter 6), but in the long run an injection of 'fresh blood' is expedient to counteract the danger of an accumulation of inherited defects. This is avoided in many primates by young males being forced to leave home and pursue their sexual careers elsewhere with unrelated females. However, in chimpanzees, maintaining the balance between in- and outbreeding is the female's responsibility.

For food, chimpanzees depend mostly on fruit that is borne on trees sporadically distributed throughout their domain. Jungles are complex environments, so these apes need an intimate knowledge of the forest to be able to exploit food such as figs as they ripen at different times. A solitary ape would be hard pressed to search a sufficient area, but the loose troops into which chimps organize themselves can cover a much greater expanse of forest to monitor their favourite larders. For intelligent apes, living socially has the added benefit of facilitating the exchange of information between the members of the troop, so that when a well-laden tree is discovered, all of the chimps get to know about it and gather for a collective banquet.

These forest apes live in mixed-sex troops of up to a hundred. Whereas females emigrate to neighbouring groups when they reach puberty, their brothers stay in their mother's troop, so they get to know every inch of the forest. Eventually, they team up with the mature but thuggish males. These are always engaged in a power struggle with each other, from which emerges an élite gang of brothers or half-brothers which lord it over the rest. They defend the troop's territory from neighbouring gangs and restlessly patrol their fiefdom, testing the reproductive state of their 'wives'. The females have sex appeal only at the height of oestrus, signified by an enlarged, flushed bottom and extremely solicitous behaviour. But not every male chimp gets an equal chance to fertilize them.

OVERLEAF Not just a pretty face. A female hamadryas baboon, like those of many primates, solicits as a form of appeasement. She can barter sex to help her get what she wants.

The establishment of a male hierarchy ensures that the leader takes precedence in sex – a situation likely to cause insurrection in the ranks. But the top male needs to retain the loyalty of his companions, especially for gang warfare. To keep them 'sweet', he allows them access to receptive females before or after he has finished with them. Less assertive and younger males on the fringes of the ruling élite are excluded from the fun, but a couple of options are open to them. Firstly, a subordinate can ingratiate himself with a top male by siding with him in petty disputes with the rest of the troop. As a favour, he might be allowed a few copulations, even during the peak of a female's fertile period. His second ploy is to risk eloping into the forest with a female which prefers gentler lovers – as some do – stay with her for a few days and mate with her. Secrecy is essential because, if discovered, he is likely to be beaten up.

A female chimpanzee generally prefers to mate with the most macho males in her troop, often screaming encouragement while they line up to copulate – it is her way of stimulating competition between them. When mating with a subordinate male, however, she hides from the view of the dominant one and suppresses her copulation call, so as to reduce the risk of violent reprisals. Recent research on a group of chimpanzees inhabiting the Tai Forest on the Ivory Coast of West Africa has revealed that many oestrous chimps are engaged in sneaky 'outbreeding'; over half of them disappeared temporarily from their home area and, according to the results of DNA fingerprinting, became impregnated by males from neighbouring communities. For females, this is a highly risky strategy because males may batter to death babies conceived by 'foreigners' – it is not in their genetic interest to protect infants to which they are not related. However, when these roving females returned to their troop and gave birth, their offspring survived, so the assignations must have been conducted with the utmost secrecy. Should any of these male 'bastards' breed, they might inject valuable fresh qualities into the troop.

Sex to keep the peace

Few large mammals can compete with the virility of male lions; one courting couple was monitored continuously in the Serengeti for two and a half days and they mated 157 times with an average interval of twenty-one minutes between sessions. Such relentless intimacy is the price of living peacefully in prides.

The most sociable of the big cats, lions live in groups of up to a dozen or more females and their cubs, with as many as four ferocious males in their prime. The latter are dangerous beasts, frequently roaring challenges to others and quite capable of causing mayhem in their own prides and slaughtering lionesses and cubs alike. But males also have a problem, because a single animal stands no chance of retaining a group of lionesses. Success in sex therefore depends upon several males – usually brothers – teaming up to topple other bands of brothers and taking over their prides. Once in power, the males must stay on friendly terms with each other to defend their harems from outsiders, so murderous competition between them for oestrous females must be prevented. The lionesses control the sexual tension of their awesome guardians and keep them loyal both to themselves and to each other by being utterly wanton with all the pride males.

Lionesses within a pride are usually sisters or half-sisters but unrelated to the shaggy-maned males. They need the warrior males to exclude neighbouring groups from the large expanse of savannah which the lionesses need for hunting. Apart from brief periods when they need to stalk and kill to eat, lionesses enjoy a relaxed way of life, spending most of the time sprawled out asleep. However, this tranquillity comes to an abrupt end when they become sexually receptive.

For three days, a lioness in heat becomes unashamedly seductive, repeatedly seeking out the males, rubbing and rolling sensuously in front of them and presenting her haunches. The most dominant member of the brotherhood takes precedence and devotes his entire energies to satisfying the lioness's sexual demands as she calls on him to straddle her raised rump nearly a hundred times a day. After a day or two, the initial male loses his enthusiasm for mating and is supplanted by one or more of his fresher brothers. This sexual athleticism plays a crucial role in keeping the peace. A lioness in oestrus can satisfy all her consorts and, as each of them copulates with her so many times, none of the males can be sure of the identity of the father – or fathers – of her next litter of cubs. However, as the alliance is generally composed of brothers, all the males will be related in varying degrees to the offspring. This uncertainty over paternity means that the males' best option is to let all the cubs live!

After as little as two or three years, the stability enjoyed by the lionesses is shattered when their protectors are supplanted by a cohort of younger males. This may happen after an unsettling period of roaring and bloody fighting in which some contestants may be badly mauled or killed. The interests of the sexes are suddenly far apart and treachery is in the air. The new males are eager to make their reproductive mark and, as they are not connected to the young produced by the vanquished brothers, they set about murdering any cubs that are still dependent on their mothers. The lionesses have already invested time and

OVERLEAF Punctuated peace. A pride of lions may look like a cohesive family but there are underlying tensions between the sexes, and between the males, which could shatter the peace. Every two or three years, murderous chaos breaks out.

effort in their offspring and do their best to hide and save them; after a takeover, some mothers may leave the pride with their cubs in order to protect them from newly victorious males. Those which stay are fairly helpless against the brutal power of their new guardians. After their litters have been killed, the lionesses come into oestrus, allowing the recent arrivals to start fathering their own families. However, lionesses from newly taken-over prides frequently and deliberately generate conflict between their fresh partners by offering themselves to any passing males. This behaviour might be to test the new coalition, to make sure that it is powerful enough to fend off intruders and ensure a two- or three-year period of peace in which each lioness can rear several litters of cubs. The teasing stops when the males have proved themselves to be the winning team.

The scorched grasslands and woodland savannahs of Africa, with their herds of watchful and fleet-footed game, have proved something of a challenge to large predators. Lions have mastered the situation through teamwork. By hunting in co-ordinated groups, they are able to capture and dispatch prey beyond the capability of lone predators. Consequently, each member of the pride profits from being social by consuming more bountiful meals of flesh from victims like zebra and Cape buffalo, and ultimately rearing larger litters, with perhaps a little sisterly help.

Matriarchal molerats

Societies can be thought of as solutions fashioned by the processes of evolution which allow animals to exploit some aspect of their surroundings. Some are very strange indeed. In Africa, there is an almost unbelievably bizarre mammal which is able to live in unforgiving environments by virtue of teamwork carried out under matriarchal control.

Naked molerats are adapted to surviving in soil which is as hard as concrete for much of the year. As their name suggests, these sightless rodents have no fur and resemble pink, animated cocktail sausages that move by wriggling along on their stubby little legs. The most noticeable feature of their grotesque bodies is a shovel-shaped mouth with enormously protruding incisor teeth, which they put to dramatic use when gnashing their way through soil. Occurring in the arid regions of Somalia, East and Southern Africa, naked molerats form colonies, each occupying a complex labyrinth of burrows which include main 'highways' linking storage depots, toilet chambers and a spacious nursery where the babies are tended. The network may well exceed 3 kilometres (2 miles) in length and enables these creatures to tackle nutritious roots and tubers at the work face in safety, concealed from the prying eyes of predators. These supplies must be harvested and stored during the very short periods of abundant rainfall which so soaks the ground that it becomes soft enough to excavate. The operation might entail the removal of several tonnes of spoil in a matter of days, and that is why these and a few other kinds of molerat live in working communities with a rudimentary caste system which, uniquely for mammals, mimics the social insects.

Barely one in a hundred naked molerats ever gets to breed. This is the privilege of the most dominant female – the queen – which together with about three males, are the only ones which are reproductively active. At 60 grams (2 ounces), the queen is double the weight of a celibate worker and devotes herself to rearing and suckling pups in the nursery chamber. Whenever she is ready to mate, she has a limited choice of mates – probably her own sons. Inbreeding does not seem to be a problem with these creatures. The queen's monopoly of sex may last a long time because, in captivity, breeding females have been known to live twenty-one years.

Although it might be advantageous for her offspring to try and break away from the nest and start their own families, the queen's extreme bossiness keeps the vast majority of her family at home and sexless. Indeed, such a community could only function through the ruthless suppression of sexual tensions. The matriarch does this by literally walking over her sons and daughters, nudging and shoving them around whenever she meets them. The constant chivvying causes stress, which in turn prevents the gonads of her offspring from maturing and keeps them occupied with the 'housework'. Should the queen die, the sudden alleviation of bullying enables a few of the heavier females to come into breeding condition; they then fight for supremacy among themselves until one prevails and becomes queen.

The queen could not survive without a massive group of miners whose job is to extend the tunnels rapidly during the brief wet seasons. She can achieve this only by enslaving both her sons and her daughters. The odds are heavily stacked against these subordinate creatures setting up their own subterranean communities in the dreadfully dry places where they live. So it is better for them to propagate some of their genes by assisting their mother to rear more sisters and brothers.

Paper wasps – co-operation and conflict

The ultimate expression of females battling among themselves for reproductive supremacy is found in the social insects. One can only marvel at the complexity of the communities found in bees, wasps and ants. In all of them, the nest is the focus of their co-operative lifestyle. It helps them make the best use of local resources, acting as a place to shelter, a nursery and a storage depot for the food they collect in the surrounding countryside. Being crucial

LEFT Trampling the opposition underfoot. A queen naked mole rat literally squashes and bullies her workers so much they are too stressed for sex.

RIGHT Chemical control: a queen bee attempts to influence her virgin daughters by giving them a special substance for which they crave. They surround her to receive their 'fix' by licking her body and by mouth to mouth contact.

to the survival of every member of the group, the nest must be defended, which requires teamwork of a high order. But this appears to be incompatible with unrestricted sex. In insect societies, there are very few winners in the battle for breeding dominance – males are marginalized and most females are forced by their mothers into becoming non-reproductive workers.

There are different levels of sophistication among wasp societies, ranging from the more or less solitary to species which live in vast colonies. Paper wasps build relatively simple nests which support quite small colonies. World wide in their distribution, they construct their delicate stalked structures of chewed wood fibres not only on twigs, but also under the sheltered eaves of buildings. As the polygonal cells are not enclosed by a protective envelope, the wasp's behaviour is fully exposed to the outside world. At first sight, the colonies seem to be models of smoothly operating societies with an egg-laying queen tended by 'sterile' workers which collect food and generally look after the nest and its brood. However, a closer examination of each colony reveals as much conflict as co-operation.

When a female wasp struggles free from her cocoon, she has the potential to become either a queen or a worker. Her final role depends partly on when she emerges.

A paper wasp's nest is generally established during the spring through the efforts of several sisters which hatched at the end of the previous summer, mated and survived the winter ready to start a new colony. However, as soon as a few cells have been constructed, the sisters start to quarrel as each strives to establish her own monopoly over egg-laying. The contestants wrestle, bite and sting each other, often falling to the ground in the fracas. As the wasps vary in size, the biggest generally ends up as the sole reigning queen. From then on, she maintains the upper hand by consuming all eggs other than her own and bullying the other foundresses, which in turn hassle the queen's offspring – the workers – which appear as the colony expands. A strict pecking order is thus enforced by the queen, causing the ovaries of her subordinate sisters and daughters to wither; they then become nurserymaids, catching caterpillars and other prey and bringing them back to the comb for the growing grubs. Ranking order also determines the succession. Should some misfortune befall the queen, the leading foundress takes over her role within about three hours, and her ovaries begin to reactivate so that she can produce her own eggs.

The extreme co-operation found in ants, bees and wasps is thought to be due to the peculiar genetic relationships that mothers, daughters and sons have with each other. A queen bee controls the sex of her offspring by the simple expedient of laying two kinds of eggs; those which are unfertilized become males, whereas females come from fertilized eggs. This method of sex determination has surprising consequences. The queen's daughters (i.e. the 'sterile' workers and future sexual queens) are significantly more closely related to each other than they are to their own female offspring. As a strategy for disseminating their genes, it is therefore more advantageous for the workers to co-operate with their mother – the queen – to rear more sisters than to produce their own daughters. This odd scenario explains why wasps and bees have evolved such apparently altruistic societies based on hugely reproductive 'mothers' and supported by vast workforces of virgin daughters, with males reduced to a minority caste of sexual studs.

And yet, there is a further genetic asymmetry in the relationship between males and females. Coming from unfertilized eggs, the drones inherit all of their genes from their mother, but females inherit theirs equally from both their parents. Female workers are therefore much less closely related to their drone brothers than they would be to their own sons. If worker bees and wasps could breed, they would favour the rearing of their own sons instead of slavishly looking after the queen's drones. This is precisely what worker honey-bees attempt to do! In paper wasps, the queen can easily dominate every one of her small brood and prevent the females from breeding. But in the honey-bee, a single queen cannot possibly physically suppress every one of her vast number of daughters – the colony is far too large – and so the scene is set for rebellion.

Rebellion in the hive

Although we know more about the honey-bee than we do about almost any other kind of insect, understanding the sexual politics of the hive is one of the most difficult areas of biology. Therefore any interpretation of what is in the queen's interest, and how this weighs against the vested interests of different factions of her workers, must be somewhat speculative. But of one thing we can be certain – honey-bees are immensely successful insects, and the key to their success is their ability to form huge, perennial colonies involving a smoothly operating labour force for flower shopping over wide areas.

Unlike paper wasps, the queen honey-bee never starts a colony by herself – she is always accompanied by a big retinue to care for her every need. On her nuptial flight, her internal storage sacs were filled with about 7 million sperm, sufficient for a career of egg production – one a minute or 3000 a day, equivalent to twice her body weight. Over the course of her three-year lifespan she makes an incredible 1,500,000 offspring and all of them are potentially at odds with her! But in this genetic conflict, the queen just manages to stay ahead of her rebellious subjects.

She attempts to control her family with a 'chemical fix' – a secretion from the glands in her mandibles (jaws) called 'queen substance' – which is distributed throughout the colony by licking and mouth-to-mouth feeding. This prevents her daughters from constructing enlarged royal brood cells for rearing new queens which might challenge her position, at least until her chemical influence begins to wane.

Even so, her working offspring are not completely subservient to their mother; they have their own agendas, caused by the different degrees of relatedness between the sexes, and between the queen and her daughters. As with paper wasps, a female worker honey-bee shares more genes with her sisters than she does with her brothers. The worker's genetic interests are therefore best served by helping her mother produce fertilized eggs rather than eggs destined to produce drones. From the queen's point of view, the reproductive value of sons and daughters should be similar. However, the workers manipulate their mother's output by preparing nursery cells that favour a mostly female brood: the majority of the cells are especially shaped for receiving the fertilized eggs that will become female. The queen can detect the difference between 'drone' and 'worker' cells by measuring the width of the open ends with her mandibles. Despite the bias in the cells with which she is confronted, she frequently retaliates by depositing unfertilized 'male' eggs into 'female' brood cells, a tactic that workers on nursery duty are programmed to counter by consuming them, as they do not want to raise brothers.

Some workers even rebel against their mother's monopoly of reproduction by developing active ovaries and secretly slipping their own eggs into the vacant brood cells. As the worker females are not inseminated, the eggs delivered can produce only drones carrying only the mother's genes. Now it is the turn of the queen to strike back; if her daughter's drones are allowed to live, they will rival the queen's own sons in the race to inseminate any new virgin queens. So, if she discovers rogue eggs which fail to bear her personal scent signature, she destroys them – thereby furthering the interests of her own male offspring, which bear only her genes.

But the queen has a final card to play in this genetic war which sets sister against sister! Some of the honey-bees engaged in policing the fresh comb will destroy their sisters' 'drone' eggs. The clue to this puzzling behaviour lies in the wildly promiscuous nature of the queen on her honeymoon. During that brief but frenetic flight she may have been mated by up to thirty unrelated sex-crazed drones, all of which managed to leave some of their sperm inside her. The eggs destined to produce workers are therefore fertilized randomly inside the queen by a cocktail of sperm from a variety of males. So, although all the workers in a colony share the queen's genes, their paternity is likely to be mixed. Rather than a single sisterhood, a honey-bee's workforce is a community of several different sisterhoods, each tracing its lineage to one or other of the drones which mated with their mother. This acts as a significant limiting influence on the degree of altruism among the workers. Although there is a beneficial genetic pay-off to sisters helping each other, half-sisters are much less likely to work together because they share fewer genes. In the case of the rogue eggs, the bees on nursery duty may be unable to distinguish whether they have been deposited by a sister or half-sister; refusing to give the eggs the benefit of the doubt, they eat them, leaving the queen's monopoly of drone production almost intact. A few escape detection and produce drones less related to the queen's sons.

Sex allocation

The ability to determine the gender of offspring is a valuable weapon in the battle of the sexes. Much recent research has revealed that many creatures do change the odds in favour of sons or daughters depending upon the circumstances. For many kinds of invertebrates, fishes and reptiles, sex can be determined by something as simple as the temperature at which an egg is incubated. For example, in turtles, eggs buried in sunny spots on the beach develop into females, whereas those interred in the shade, where the sand is cooler, produce males. The sex ratio sometimes varies even within a single clutch, with females hatching from the warmer eggs near the surface and males emerging from those at the bottom of the nest.

Sons and daughters do not always have the same reproductive value to a parent – the same is true of some human societies – and so, in some situations, it pays the mother to skew the proportion in favour of one or the other sex. The classic example is provided by the tiny fig wasp. The mother injects her eggs into the central cavity of the fruit, and as with bees, she fertilizes only some of them to produce females; the others make males. On hatching, the offspring breed incestuously inside the fig, the brothers fighting each other for the privilege of inseminating their sisters. After-wards, they all leave through a minute pore in the top of the fruit, incidentally carrying the fig's pollen. However, the founding mother can allocate sex to her offspring and alter the ratio depending upon whether other fig wasps have already deposited their eggs or not. If the fig is free of other broods, producing lots of sons is a waste

because just a few would suffice to inseminate many females. Under these circumstances, she produces about one son for every ten daughters, which maximizes the reproductive potential of her family. However, if the fruit already contains eggs from other fig wasps, then she produces lots of unfertilized eggs destined to produce a surfeit of sons to compete for mates with males from other broods.

Boy or girl? The sex of a spotted hyena's pups can be influenced by the environment. In times of plenty, females are preferred.

In birds and mammals, sex is determined genetically – maleness in mammals is due to a single gene carried on a special chromosome called the 'Y', which is passed on by half of the father's sperm, thus accounting for a 50:50 sex ratio. However, there is evidence that some female mammals and birds can, by an unknown mechanism, nudge the sex ratio of their offspring one way or the other. In a classic study of red deer on the Scottish island of Rhum, it was noticed that high-status hinds in the pink of condition were giving birth to rather more sons than daughters. Furthermore, these mothers were blessed with more grandchildren by their sons than by their daughters. On the other hand, hinds of low status were producing more daughters than sons and, although they had fewer grandchildren than the dominant females, what grandchildren they did produce were more likely to be born to their daughters than sired by their male offspring. In these and other cases, mothers seemed to favour whichever sex was likely to result in the highest number of descendants. In red deer, the discovery that the hind's rank and condition affected the breeding career of her offspring made sense of the differential sex ratio. Sons raised by socially dominant hinds in good health got a good start in life. They grew into robust, assertive stags which secured their own harems and sired far more youngsters than a perfectly healthy female could ever rear. A low-ranking mother, perhaps harassed and undernourished, could at best give birth to weak and scrawny sons with little prospect of becoming breeding stags. For such a mother, daughters were a better investment because, regardless of their condition, they were likely to become pregnant and continue the line.

Extremely skewed sex ratios are somehow achieved in Seychelles warblers, and the quality of the parents' nesting area affects whether there is a preponderance of males or females. If the environment is rich in food, a pair of these boringly brown birds hatch up to 87 per cent daughters – the sex which is retained as 'helpers' (see later in this chapter) – whereas in poorer places, they produce 77 per cent sons, which tend to disperse. This shift in sex ratios has been elegantly demonstrated by translocating pairs from high- to low-quality territories and vice versa. It seems that when daughters are able to assist their parents to rear further broods, they are cranked out in preference to sons, but when they can only hinder by competing with their parents for food they are underproduced in preference to sons which fly away from home. Exactly how the hen Seychelles warblers have such a control over sex allocation remains a mystery.

For social creatures, the capacity to influence the gender of their offspring is a powerful 'tool' because it gives females the ability to shape the sexual composition of groups to their own advantage. Astonishingly, female spotted hyenas are able to manipulate the sexual bias of their offspring according to circumstances. For most of the time, daughters are desirable, but when conditions turn bad, sons are selected.

Although hyenas can survive as solitary scavengers, they generally live in clans consisting of a hierarchy of related females, dominated by one very assertive individual. The wimpish males are in the minority, possess little status and generally cower on the edges of the groups where they defer to the 'butch' females and their small offspring. The spotted hyenas' lifestyle enables individuals to profit from the co-operative defence of their hunting territory and through teamwork they are able to bring down large prey such as wildebeest and zebra. When successful, their kills attract distant members of the clan and perhaps lions and jackals as well, so more often than not a scrimmage develops in which the spoils are keenly fought over. Such competition for a share of the food might explain why female spotted hyenas are much larger and more aggressive than males, because they must fight to feed well in order to support their young families.

When the hunting is good, hyenas give birth to an overwhelming majority of female cubs – for every male born into the clan, there may be as many as fifteen females. This has survival value for the females, because the production of too many males is a waste of resources; they scoff food which could be usefully consumed by mothers, and cannot wet-nurse their offspring. They are of value only as studs and a few of those can satisfy many females. Daughters, on the other hand, can hunt, guard and generate more reproductive females to enlarge the pack and make it invincible.

It seems a more detailed explanation of the female's behaviour is called for. In some senses she is an 'honorary male' and this is clearly advantageous to her. The brawnier she is, the more likely she is to end up at the top of the clan. Together with her female companions, she will be able to defend the core area of the territory more effectively from outsiders, to run faster, disable prey more quickly and win a better place at the 'table' in the face of intense feeding competition. Her stomach will be more capacious and, when it is full, this will enhance her ability to fuel her milk supply, thereby giving her pups a better chance of surviving. Unlike lionesses, which will suckle one another's offspring, the mother hyena alone shoulders the burden of providing for her pups. As rank in spotted hyena clans is inherited, the daughters which she produces will be dominant and one of them will probably succeed her at the top of the hierarchy. The pay-off for high status is therefore considerable, because the matriarch will probably raise twice as many young as her subordinate companions. To achieve this, her body is flooded with androgens – male sex hormones – to give her the characteristics of an aggressive super-male. And as if to demonstrate her superior dominance, the female hyena has evolved the very emblems of maleness.

Curious though it may seem, it is almost impossible to tell the sex of a spotted hyena by looking at its anatomy. Although a male has all the normal accoutrements of his gender, the female is pure burlesque. Beneath her anus hangs a sham scrotum filled with fibrous tissue, and a much elongated clitoris dangles from just below her vaginal opening. This organ is of similar size and structure to the male's penis, but the similarity is further enhanced by the fact that the female can erect it in a display of rank whenever she encounters another member of her clan.

The masculinization of the genitalia causes a female difficulties when she gives birth for the first time, because the pups have to pass down a greatly elongated birth canal which incorporates an acute bend leading to the enlarged clitoris. Labour often takes several hours to give the sham penis time to accommodate the foetus as it squeezes through. In the end, the tube generally tears, but sometimes not before the pup has been lodged inside for half an hour on the end of a detached placenta, causing it to suffocate. A contributory factor is the large size of the pups. Under the influence of massive exposure to male hormones while inside their mother's uterus, young hyenas are born with a pugilistic streak and fight so seriously among themselves that sometimes only a single victorious youngster survives to monopolize its mother's attention. Accordingly, big and precocious foetuses have evolved because they will be stronger fighters at birth. The suckling period is especially long because, unlike African wild dogs and wolves, in which both sexes regurgitate half-digested flesh for their pups, spotted hyenas rarely return to their den with food. The young are weaned only slowly on to a more solid diet and are not completely independent of their mother's milk until they are well over a year old.

Pure burlesque. The genitals of a female spotted hyena look similar to a male's. To demonstrate her superior dominance, the female has developed the emblems of maleness.

Should prolonged drought or disease make it difficult for the members of the clan to rear their cubs, the dominant female produces sons rather than daughters. This makes perfect sense in that daughters always stick close to their mothers and the appearance of more of them at a time when the clan needs to contract would be counter-productive. Young males, on the other hand, leave their mother's territory and join other clans. When life gets hard, it therefore pays female spotted hyenas to invest in sons, which will not compete for dwindling food supplies with their parents. As an added bonus, the young males may settle down and mate with females in neighbouring clans, thereby maintaining the parental line.

Co-operation – sex deferred

Animals which, for whatever reason, live in permanent but related groups tend to evolve clear roles to the benefit of everyone in the group. This leads inevitably to co-operative lifestyles in which sexual conflict is largely abandoned, especially when each individual has a genetic stake in the offspring. The acorn woodpecker is an icon of such communal living. The breeding core of the group may contain any combination of cocks and hens, from a conventional monogamous couple and their offspring helpers, to arrangements with multiple partners of either sex.

With black and white bodies and scarlet crowns, acorn woodpeckers are pretty inhabitants of ancient oak woodlands of the American west. Drawing attention to themselves by their bounding flights and excited calling from the canopies, these gregarious birds have unbelievably complex societies. As their name suggests, they have a zeal for collecting acorns, which are then stored in the trunks of particular trees. Many of these larders have been in use for generations and are among the wonders of nature; some have tens of thousands of holes bored into their branches to accommodate the acorns on which the birds rely to survive the lean winter months. Acorn woodpeckers live in large, squabbling families in which only a small proportion of the adults breed. The rest of the entourage – the offspring and non-breeding adults – forms an avian co-op to hoard the crucially important acorns. A healthy store just tips the balance between starvation and staying alive during the winter, and so the extended family needs to pull together to harvest as many acorns as possible during the autumn. However, when spring arrives, the helpers stay on to assist the breeders in realizing their reproductive potential. Why should they do so?

The effort of chiselling out a nesting chamber in the hard wood of an oak is so demanding that first-summer birds are unlikely to prepare a satisfactory nest, so ready-made ones are extremely desirable and have a very high 'second-hand' value.

It therefore pays the offspring of acorn woodpeckers to stay at home until they see even a faint chance of taking over their parents' nest. Until then, they bide their time, toiling to build a winter store and servicing the needs of the breeding birds. The parents profit from assistance with nursery duty and the helpers gain by proxy, improving the survival rate of their brothers and sisters, nephews and nieces, all of which harbour some of their own genes.

But within this arena of co-operation there is tension, because being a slave is always second-best. Two key events in the acorn woodpecker's life bear witness to the social stress. At laying time, hens break any eggs deposited early by other hens, but stop as soon as they start to lay themselves, presumably because they cannot then distinguish one egg from another. However, this bizarre behaviour results in clutches from several hens hatching simultaneously and, from the point of view of the egg-smashers, guarantees that their own offspring will benefit from the helpers' efforts, which peak when there are most chicks in the nest chamber. Overtly, this may look like co-operation, but it is really the outcome of a bitchy battle!

The second major expression of conflict occurs either when a breeding space becomes vacant – perhaps through death – or when a helper makes an assertive bid to establish itself as a breeder. An impressive power struggle then ensues in which the breeding birds resist the challenge of their progeny, presumably as a defence against inbreeding. However, the general turmoil almost immediately attracts helpers from neighbouring groups, which enter the fray for the prize breeding position; one or more of them is far more likely to succeed.

Acorn woodpeckers are therefore destined for a life of family feuding until they see an opportunity open up in neighbouring territories – and then, arguably, the real battle has just started. The alternative is to prospect a fresh site and hammer out a new home, but the chances of success are low, with the continual risk of being usurped by another.

Chicknappers of the Australian bush

Acorn woodpeckers illustrate beautifully how competition for a resource which is extremely valuable – in their case, nest sites – lends itself to co-operative behaviour. But it is not just breeding places which are necessary. Some animals manage to eke out a living where food itself is sparse, and this encourages the evolution of a remarkable degree of co-operation. A bird which has been driven down this route occurs in the Australian outback.

White-winged choughs are unexceptional-looking, crow-sized insect-eaters of the eucalyptus woodlands of eastern Australia, where they forage on the ground in flocks of up to twenty individuals. Their unique domestic arrangements are forced on them by the fact that a pair would find it impossible to raise any offspring at all without a lot of assistance.

Being a white-winged chough is far from easy. The birds have great difficulty discovering enough food and this fact is central to our understanding of their communal existence. In the dry eucalyptus bush, hunting for insects is labour intensive because the habitat lacks the distinct seasonal peaks of productivity which, elsewhere, tend to stimulate breeding. Without marked flushes of flowers or foliage, and the insects that depend upon them, the adult choughs can only just keep themselves alive, let alone unearth a sufficient surplus to feed a crop of nestlings. In practice, it takes the combined efforts of about seven individuals to raise a single chick. Those assisting the parents are enlisted as juveniles; rather than dispersing after fledging, they stay home for several years. During this time, they muck in to build the arboreal mud nest, and take turns incubating the eggs, guarding the brood and bringing the nestlings food. Although most songbirds are fully grown by the time they are a year old, white-winged choughs continue to gain weight until their fifth year, when they finally become sexually mature. During their growing phase, they sometimes cheat on their tasks by pretending to put a nourishing morsel into a nestling's gape and then slyly swallowing it themselves – something that the parents never do!

The sheer difficulty of discovering food may be the reason for the choughs deferring the onset of sexual maturity. It pays young birds to stay with their parents as long as possible to learn how to forage in these low-yielding woodlands. By trial and error and by watching the experienced adults, the youngsters steadily improve their feeding efficiency – which may take about three years. Even at this age, they are incapable of supporting their own families, so it is in both their and their parents' interests to contribute to the group's breeding success. Once their gonads are functional, the young adult choughs aspire to breeding themselves, but they might have a long wait until they can take over their parents' domain when one or other of them dies, or lead a splinter group when the family fragments.

When the family increases to fifteen or more individuals, it usually splits into several factions. The older helpers now become imbued with sexual passion and fight for dominance, forging alliances with a few friendly siblings to constitute their own viable breeding groups. The diminished families may enhance their strength with extra helpers from neighbouring groups by 'chicknapping'. Squabbles between the adjoining families occur almost daily, and each one defends its own fledglings from thieving neighbours. Even nestlings are targeted, the trespassing team coaxing one or more

LEFT Helper at the nest: an Australian white-winged chough forgoes breeding for several years in order to help its parents to rear some more brothers and sisters, with whom it shares some of its own genes.

OPPOSITE Upwardly mobile: a baby baboon rides on the back of its older brother. The status of a young monkey depends upon the rank of its mother and on currying favour with the big boys.

youngsters from its mud nursery while the parental group is kept at bay. Once on the ground, the little fluttering creatures are shepherded into the neighbour's territory, where they are reared as helpers. Unfortunately, not all victims of chicknapping survive.

Helpers are found in a number of different kinds of animal. Among mammals, kinkajous, jackals, meerkats and mongooses retain members of their family for various 'domestic' purposes. Dwarf mongooses go around in packs consisting of a single breeding pair and their offspring. Hunting by daylight, they are vulnerable to eagles, so each individual benefits from the combined alertness of many pairs of eyes. The members of the troop assist their parents by baby-sitting and the females wet-nurse their baby brothers and sisters. In Lake Tanganyika there is even a cichlid fish, called *Lamprologus brichardi*, whose offspring hang around to help protect their younger siblings. However, they have been seen to 'cheat' by eating the eggs when their parents are away from 'home'!

Bonobos – the erotic ape

Sex has been very much a source of stress in all of the animal communities so far touched upon in this chapter. In complete contrast, another ape – the bonobo – shows extraordinary behaviour which echoes our own culture, much of which is sexually orientated. Far from being reserved only for top males and therefore divisive, bonobo sex is for all.

Tolerance seems to be achieved by allowing sex between consenting apes whenever they want it! Even the juveniles indulge in erotic games. There seems to be only one taboo – when males are more than six years old, they do not mate with their mothers. What benefit bonobo society derives from such wanton promiscuity is by no means clear, except that sex appears to be a socially cohesive activity.

Discovered just over sixty years ago, the bonobo is the least well known of the four great apes. Once called the pygmy chimpanzee – a misnomer because it is similar in size to its better known cousin – it is by far the sexiest of the apes. Bonobos differ from chimpanzees in being born with black – not pink – faces and hands, in possessing small ears which are concealed behind side whiskers, and in the adults retaining a tuft of white hair where you would expect to see a tail. Unfortunately, the survival of these intriguing animals must be considered precarious because they live only in remote equatorial forests in the Democratic Republic of Congo (formerly Zaire), one of the most politically turbulent parts of the world.

Few scientists have so far been privileged to observe bonobos in the wild, but those who have could be forgiven for thinking that they have sex eternally on their minds. Like us, but unlike chimpanzees, this amazing ape practises far more recreational than reproductive sex. The most striking thing about the bonobos' boundless sexuality is that they use any excuse to engage each other in a variety of sexual practices with little regard for gender, age or social status. Males mount females at any stage of the menstrual cycle and females sometimes mount them back; females embrace and stare into each other's eyes while vigorously rubbing their swollen pink genitals together, and males stand rump to rump and press their scrotal sacs together while grinning and screaming with apparent pleasure; adults of both sexes perform acts with juveniles that we would condemn as paedophilia. Indeed, the infants and adolescents themselves play sex games; young males indulge in 'penis fencing', hanging from branches and bouncing off each other using their feet while each rubs his erect penis against his companion's. These animals are nothing if not gymnastic in their sexual techniques, sometimes masturbating or copulating while swinging from branches – no holds are barred and everyone does it with everyone else! Furthermore, there is nothing secretive about their sex – they commit acts of the greatest intimacy in front of the entire troop.

Heterosexual copulation is the only form of coupling that leads to the release of sperm. However, the kind of grimacing and vocalizations which characterize orgasm are displayed by all combinations of males and females. Almost any excuse is used to indulge in foreplay. Serious sexual sessions seem to precede, accompany or follow any socially exciting situation. For instance, a feeding assembly of bonobos often plunges into what resembles a Bacchanalian orgy.

The reason for rich and prolific sex may lie in the fact that they use it to make friends and form alliances. Like the hippies of the 1960s, bonobos make love not war. In fact, these apes are uncharacteristically peaceful. They rarely engage in physical fighting and usually resolve their differences with a charge and a swipe accompanied by a lot of screaming. Sex seems to be a 'social lubricant' – a way of diffusing tension because altercations of any kind or situations which are fraught are often accompanied by an outbreak of heterosexual and lesbian coupling. They are precisely the circumstances in which we might be expected to shake hands. However, for much of the time, the bonds of friendship between males and females, and among females, are very strong, and regular sexual relations are used to reinforce these bonds.

This is especially important for the females. Unlike most primates, whose adolescent males leave the troop into which they were born and set out on the stressful task of finding somewhere else to live, in bonobos it seems to be the females' task to join an unfamiliar troop. They use their sexual favours to help them become assimilated into new communities and build fresh friendships. Female chimpanzees achieve this by mutual grooming and searching for fruit and eating together. Female bonobos use sex. Accordingly, they maintain the erotic pink swellings on their backsides for a comparatively long time, partly concealing the moment when they ovulate during the middle of their cycle. This might keep the males guessing over the paternity of the offspring, thus ensuring that they all remain friendly. By contrast, the female chimpanzee's sex drive is locked into her menstrual cycle; once she is pregnant she is not interested in proper copulation.

The female bonobo's alliances, established and reinforced by sex, are important because they determine the pecking order at feeding sites. High-ranking females and those with high-ranking friends eat first, whereas subordinate ones may not get anything if food is scarce. Also, by banding together, female bonobos have discovered strength in numbers, and this gives them leverage over the larger and more powerful males, which would otherwise push them around. Unlike most other primates – where tensions sometimes run high between males and females, bonobo females are not afraid of males and the sexes mingle happily. Indeed, females will even trade sex for food – offering themselves to a male in return for a choice cluster of fruit in his possession! For bonobos, it seems, sex is fun and keeps the group together.

Some aspects of bonobo behaviour are very reminiscent of human sex; for example, we share varied mating positions

Bottoms and breasts

and 'make love' for enjoyment, often when there is no chance of conception taking place. But there is more. Female bonobos and women uniquely do not advertise their periods of maximum fertility, but do it differently. Whereas female bonobos appear almost permanently fertile, with a tumescent sexual skin, human females suppress all obvious clues marking their cycles of fertility. Way back, ape-women probably possessed sexual skin, but this has been lost some time during the last 5 million years of our evolution. Although we can only speculate as to the reason, the loss may be connected with our upright stance; the bulbous genital areas used to signal sexual availability and fertility may have made it awkward to walk when our human ancestors began to stand upright. Perhaps such swellings were replaced by enlarged hairless buttocks – permanent signs of sexiness – which became echoed on the chest by a pair of bulbous breasts. Their shape is unconnected with milk production – lactating chimpanzees and

LEFT Wild and wanton, bonobo chimps are the epitome of sexual freedom. Here two females rub their genitals, coupling pleasure with social cohesion.

RIGHT Sitting on the evidence: female gelada baboons indicate their sexual readiness by red patches on their breasts which mimic their bottoms and glow brightly when they are receptive. The male (right) has a similar red patch.

gorillas are relatively flat chested. In our own species, the mammary glands are surrounded by much fatty tissue – in fact, two-thirds of the human breast is simply padding to make them stand out from the chest. One explanation is that breasts evolved as erotic signals, effective in frontal amorous encounters. Evidence for this explanation comes from the gelada baboon, which also displays such a 'genital echo'.

Another name for this monkey is the 'bleeding heart baboon'. Both sexes possess an hour-glass-shaped area of naked red skin on their chests. However, the female provides the clue as to the significance of the raw-looking patch, because it bears an uncanny resemblance to her sexual skin, blushing and swelling in beat with her menstrual cycle. Even the central position of her pendulous nipples is a passable imitation of her vulva. But why should she possess a mock sexual skin on her chest? The habits of the species may provide the answer: geladas spend much of their time squatting on their haunches. They even sit down while they are feeding, so concealing the most important focus for sexual signalling – their posterior. By evolving a voluptuous rump pattern on their chests, where it is easily displayed, the females have solved the problem.

The question arises as to why human females should conceal their best time for conceiving. Perhaps this is yet another consequence of the battle of the sexes. Any ape-woman 'on heat' would be likely to inflame male passions and possibly be a target for their aggression. By failing to reveal the time of ovulation – either behaviourally or by some outward sign – they might prevent the males from fighting over them and so escape being beaten up. Concealed ovulation might also have been a ploy to keep the loyalty of the menfolk, who needed to guard their females and copulate regularly to ensure their paternity.

What use are men?

So, apart from injecting sperm, what use are men? Rearing a hominid child involves an arduous commitment over a dozen or more years before it stands a chance of becoming independent. This protracted period of childhood is due to our enormous brains, which require a long time to grow and function effectively. Among our primate relatives, rearing is female business, but the task of bringing up a succession of infants is beyond the ability of lone hominid mothers; the problem is that once one is weaned, the mother can become pregnant again, but the older children will still need her or other adults to supply them with food for several years. It was traditionally thought that male hominids acted as providers for their wives and offspring in aboriginal societies. The men were powerfully built and specialized as hunters, heroically 'bringing home the bacon' to the women, who spent their days gathering plant food and caring for the children.

However, this picture of co-operation between the sexes may well be a travesty of what really happened in our past. A careful analysis of the contributions made by men and women in modern tribal communities reveals the truth – that women not only shoulder the burden of parenthood, but also provide far more food than the men. The occasional all-male hunting trip can certainly bring in a bonanza of meat to be shared among the members of the community, but most expeditions result in the hunters returning home empty-handed. So, in early human societies, men may have behaved like typical male mammals, shirking most of the onerous work in favour of male-bonding activities, strutting their stuff and philandering. For help in rearing the children, it seems that women might have turned to each other for reciprocal favours, rather than relying on their mates to provide for them and their young dependents. With a system of co-wives in place for wet-nursing and generally looking after children, female hominids were free to have a succession of offspring. For aboriginal men, the pay-off came with the enhanced status of being a reputedly successful hunter – it brought a bonus of sexual opportunities. Although an aboriginal woman might have been left with a less than ideal man for a partner, she might also have enjoyed having a good hunter as a neighbour, accepting his occasional gifts of meat in return for furtive sex and the chance to acquire his genes for her children.

The asymmetry in the relationship still exists. Then as now, spouses had shared objectives, but they also had divergent interests firmly rooted in their sexual biology. Today, women still bear the brunt of parental responsibility. Although there are plenty of men who work hard, are devoted and faithful husbands and dote on their children, men are far more likely than women to renege on their commitments and devote time, money and effort to status symbols, sport and sexual conquests. Even among self-styled 'happily married' working couples in North America, wives spend on average twice as many hours as their husbands on their job, caring for the children and running the home.

When so many creatures replicate themselves without resorting to this stressful, mechanically awkward method of reproducing, one might ask what the advantage of the sexual process is? In other words, is sex more trouble than it is worth?

CHAPTER

6

WHY SEX?

From the human perspective, 'why sex' seems an odd question, because we have no choice in the matter, and sex has to be more fun than budding! And yet it is a serious one which merits deeper consideration. It is today an area of exhaustive research, with many eminent minds engaged in finding a plausible answer.

Every living creature aims to achieve genetic domination by spreading as many copies of its own genes as possible. The extent to which it does so is a measure of its success. The unattainable goal is for an animal to fill the world with duplicates of itself. However, a planet literally brimming with, for example, similar bacteria or identical elephants is inconceivable and impractical – no single kind of clone could possibly survive in glorious isolation, occupying every inhabitable nook and cranny. Living things need other life forms to sustain themselves. Nevertheless, the innate 'ambition' to attain genetic glory holds true, and by far the most effective way to achieve this is to clone alone. Straightforward vegetative replication is quick and does not involve awkward interactions with other individuals. Furthermore, budding or fission has been employed by many organisms for at least 1000 million years. Yet the main thrust of evolution has been to take animals in their quest 'to populate the planet with themselves' down a much more complicated route – the sexual one.

The riddle of sex is nicely exemplified by mating slugs. Shell-less snails have quite extraordinary sexual arrangements. They are what is known as simultaneous hermaphrodites, each being endowed with a functional set of both male and female gonads. One might therefore predict that slugs would save themselves a lot of trouble by fertilizing themselves – and yet they choose not to do so. When a slug experiences the urge to breed, it slithers around for some time looking for a like-minded mate and ends up in a slimy embrace, exchanging sperm with its partner. Courtship and cross-copulation seem to be sensuous activities, the participants exploring each other's bodies while their respective penises become extremely tumescent and tightly entwined. Some species, including leopard slugs from Australia and European great grey slugs, consummate their sexual act spinning in mid-air like trapeze artists. The couples hang on the end of a tough mucous strand up to a metre (over 3 feet) long, anchored to a leaf or twig, with their coiled genitalia dangling up to 30 centimetres (12 inches) below them.

Slug sex poses a fascinating question – why mate with someone else when you could fertilize yourself? The puzzle continues because, as a method of multiplying,

PREVIOUS PAGES The riddle of slug sex: at home on the seas, blue ocean sea-slugs are killers, rasping into the flesh of stinging jellyfish. Like many molluscs, each has both male and female organs. So when they can fertilize themselves, why do they always make the sexual connection and exchange sperm with a partner, as they are doing here?

sex is often absurdly complicated and 'expensive' in the profligate expenditure of energy by the participants. Furthermore, the process compels an individual to 'throw away' half its genes while passing the other half on to its offspring. When the overriding imperative of every organism is to press as many of its own genes into the next generation as possible, why should any animal help another of the opposite sex to promulgate 50 per cent of theirs in their joint offspring? If these were the only considerations, no organism in its right mind would favour coupling with someone else to make babies and risk diluting his or her own perfectly good genetic constitution. However, the vast majority of animals and plants opt over-whelmingly for sex, for reasons which are still the subject of a great deal of speculation. Some startling revelations which have come to light in favour of sex are explored in this chapter. But first, what about the cloning?

The greatest communities on Earth are a testament to what can be achieved by ## *Cloning alternating lifestyles* breeding without the participation of separate males and females. Coral provinces such as the barrier reefs off the coasts of Australia and Belize are large enough to be observed from space, and yet they are laid down by numerous colonies of tiny polyps. Each is founded by a single individual, itself the product of an egg and sperm, which then replicates itself by repeated budding. So do the offspring. These coral clones endure for ages and can grow to be massive – like the mighty colonies of aptly named brain coral, which look like huge boulders, or the thickets of branch-ing stagshorn which may sprawl across vast areas of reef. The polyps derived from the founder member are genetically identical and are united by common tissue con-nections. Corals have another way of spreading – through pieces breaking off and establishing daughter colonies close to the parental ones. The result can often be observed in whip corals, which frequently occur in clumps, caused by small lengths of the original clone dropping to the sea-floor and commencing to grow close to the base as a thicket of small whips.

Coral polyps are also capable of multiplying by sexual means (see Chapter 3), as indeed are the related hydroids. However, these have 'split personalities', existing as two quite distinct bodies with different lifestyles – as delicate colonial polyps firmly attached like plants to some substrate, and as free-swimming sexual medusas. Branching colonies of *Obelia* and *Sertularia* are common between the tidelines adhering to rocks and seaweed. The tentacled polyps remain attached to each other by hollow stem-like connections, so that food snared and ingested by

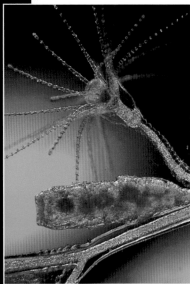

LEFT A bag of gonads.
The tiny medusa is just one
stage of a bizarre life cycle
which alternates between
asexual polyps like the one
above. The flask-like
gonotheca produces free-
swimming medusa which
carry the orange gonads.

OPPOSITE A deadly clone.
Each part of a Portuguese
man-o'-war is made up of
different polyps or 'persons'
that work as a team –
some are sensory, while
others act as mouths,
or carry the vicious stings,
or the reproductive organs.

one can be transported to the rest of the colony. Some of the polyps are shaped like flasks inside which are formed minute jellyfish that eventually swim off into the plankton. They carry the gonads on the underside of their bells, and release gametes into the sea. The fertilized eggs form larvae and these settle and grow into further colonies of polyps.

Even the larger jellyfishes of pellucid beauty are simply the most conspicuous sexual stages of a life-cycle that begins with a fertilized egg and a microscopic larva. After settling, perhaps in a rock pool or beneath a rocky overhang, it grows into a transparent polyp which eventually takes on the appearance of a stack of dinner plates less than a centimetre (½ inch) tall. The 'plates' are, in fact, tiny medusas called *ephyrae*, cloned in large numbers from the founding polyp, which break off and grow into big, pulsing jellies. The common moon jellyfish *Aurelia* is the most familiar of the marine medusas. Although each is a bag of sea water held together by the merest trace of living tissue, the four-lobed purple gonads show up through their diaphanous bells.

The Portuguese man-o'-war is an ocean-going jellyfish with a difference. This iridescent blue and pink 'galleon', which lives at the whim of winds and ocean currents, is a complex clone, but the polyps – often referred to as 'persons' – are specialized for different tasks. The sail and gas-filled bladder which keep the colony of genetically similar individuals afloat are derived from one polyp; others are modified for feeding, digesting and catching food. The latter are elongated into vivid blue tentacles that trail up to 30 metres (100 feet) behind the float, making it one of the longest animals in the world. The tentacles are studded with batteries of minute harpoons (nematocysts), which inject paralysing poison into anything that touches them. Nestling beneath the float and surrounded by sensory 'persons' is a cluster of polyps whose sole function is to generate small male and female medusas which are set free into the plankton.

Reflecting on the undoubted success of these organisms and their widespread distribution, it is impossible to castigate cloning as a strategy for reproduction. The speed by which such animals can propagate themselves is extraordinary. Nevertheless, there are big disadvantages to vegetative reproduction which stem from the fact that organisms confined to cloning cannot respond very quickly to changes in their surroundings. Sex creates more variability in each generation, and organisms practising sexual reproduction in a changing and unpredictable environment would have great advantages over those staunch individuals unable to move with the times.

When conditions are ideal, replication without sex is extremely effective at swamping the world with descendants, as any gardener who has waged war on green- or blackflies can testify. These sap-feeding aphids have evolved quite complicated

Aphids – the best of both worlds

seasonal lifestyles with alternating sexual and asexual generations, often combined with migrations from one set of host plants to another. During the spring and summer, when plants are growing fast and generating vast areas of pristine foliage and succulent new stems, the race is on between these and other sap-suckers to colonize them and exploit the riches they contain. Foremost among them are female aphids, which either hatch from eggs which have overwintered on leaf buds or fly in from other host plants on which they have survived the fallow winter months. They waste no time looking for mates or making males; under these circumstances they 'xerox' themselves by giving birth parthenogenetically to virgin daughters which are them-selves already pregnant. This telescoping of generations results in the strange fact that a mature female already has her own granddaughters developing inside her!

The potential for growth in a population of aphids is staggering. For example, under favourable conditions, a virgin peach-potato aphid, *Myzus persicae*, can give birth, sometimes in batches, to about a hundred nymphs over the course of her two- or three-week lifespan. Each will mature in ten days, so that together they will produce 10,000 granddaughters for the original mother in her brief lifetime. Theoretically, after a summer's season of about three months, the sheer weight of offspring from a female aphid would tip the scales at about 10 million tonnes!

Needless to say, the world is not inundated by an ever-expanding population of aphids, because the full reproductive potential of these insects is never realized – a host of predators have become specialists in devouring them, and ultimately a shortage of food severely curtails their breeding capacity. Nevertheless, through their ability to clone, some common kinds of aphids are able to breed sufficiently quickly to smother the tender young leaves and growing tips of their hosts. The infestations may be so heavy that they cause severe wilting, secondary fungal infections due to the amount of sugary honey dew they excrete, or disease through transmitting viruses. This is especially true of the peach-potato aphid, which attacks more kinds of plants than any other species and acts as an important carrier of diseases.

Fortunately for us, the environment rarely stays aphid-friendly for too long and, although rapid multiplication is an effective strategy to follow in benign circumstances with an expanding food supply, a different one is called for when it becomes colder and plants on which the insects feed either stop growing or die back. By autumn,

aphids need to take out insurance against unpredictable if not hazardous conditions, and this is when the females produce a generation of sexual daughters and sons. Unlike most asexual females, these are winged so that they can disperse and discover partners derived from different mothers. In producing sexual offspring, aphids sacrifice productivity while gaining the main benefit that accrues from sex – variety.

Virgin birth. A greenfly produces a tiny daughter which is already pregnant. By dispensing with sex, a single aphid could in theory quickly overwhelm the planet with her identical descendants.

Speciation – the subdividing of life forms into distinct species – is the ultimate expression of variety. It is easy to take for granted the magnificent array of animals and plants which share our world, although the stark images of empty landscapes beamed back from our neighbour Mars should be a salutary reminder of what a barren Earth would be like. Nurtured by friendly conditions with abundant water, life on our 'blue' planet exploded into a multiplicity of amazing designs. There is little doubt that the sexual process has been responsible for creating this fantastic treasury of living things, reflecting all the glorious colours of the rainbow and including us humans with our powerful brains capable of analysis and rapturous appreciation. A diversion into genetics will reveal how this has happened.

The blueprint of every individual form of life on this planet, whether a bacterium or a blue whale, is written in the genes on the

Chemical codes

chromosomes. Furthermore, all cells in the body, excepting our red blood corpuscles and gametes, contain a full complement of the genetic instructions for that individual. The amount of information that these chemical instruction manuals contain is daunting. Each human being, for instance, has around 100,000 different genes located on twenty-three pairs of chromosomes and it has been estimated that it would take about 1000 600-page volumes to write out the data. This is encoded in the molecular arrangement of special proteins called nucleic acids (DNA). When an animal such as an aphid clones, the mother's genetic manual is simply copied, so that the daughters are faithful replicas of her. However, sex deliberately rewrites the set of instructions for each offspring, and the way this happens is a miracle of biological chemistry.

An organism possesses two copies of every gene, one donated by the father and one by the mother, and these are located on each of a matched pair of chromosomes. During the formation of the sperms and eggs, a remarkable procedure called meiosis takes place inside the dividing cells; this is crucial to the sexual process, because it separates the chromosomal pairs, thereby halving the complement of genes going to each of the sex cells. A kind of molecular lottery then takes place, determining in a random fashion which copy of a gene a sperm or egg receives. Portions of chromosomes are also swapped between the complementary pairs, and errors in the replication of the DNA inevitably occur and manifest themselves as mutations or 'sports' – the blue budgerigar was originally a sport thrown up in captivity by otherwise normal green parents. There is, therefore, a great deal of shuffling and altering of the genetic pack on the sperm- and egg-production lines.

When the sex cells ultimately fuse at fertilization, their respective genes integrate to form a complete instruction pack for making a new organism, which differs not only from those of the parents, but also from those of every other individual of the species. As bodies are transient and genes – or at least copies of them – are immortal, an organism may be viewed simply as a vehicle fashioned by genes to make further DNA. This is another way of saying that a chicken is an egg's way of making more eggs!

DNA – the chemical basis of genes – is amazing stuff. The amount present in the sperm and fertilized eggs responsible for manufacturing every human being since Christ – about 16,000 million souls – would weigh less than a gram ($\frac{1}{30}$ ounce)! That is what all the human sex, passion, jealousy and lavish parental care has been about over the past 2000 years – barely a teaspoonful of DNA!

The potential of the sexual process for creativity is mind boggling. For example, it has been calculated that a human couple, given an eternity of breeding, is capable of producing five octillion (5,000,000,000,000,000,000,000,000,000) genetically different children. With this stupendous variability available to just one man and one woman through sexual reproduction, the odds on separate pregnancies resulting in identical children are too remote to contemplate. Given the number of humans, let alone the population of aphids intent upon sex at the end of the summer, the potential genetic permutations are infinite.

It is little wonder that once the sexual process appeared, evolution moved into top gear. Furthermore, males may possibly contribute more to the process than females. The reason lies in the nature of the sexes' respective gamete-production lines. Sperm-manufacturing cells divide many more times than those cells which mature into eggs. For instance, a human male makes about 100 million such cells a day, containing enough DNA to girdle the planet twice. A large number of cell divisions creates greater opportunities for errors to creep into the copying process, and some of the altered genes may be more viable than their predecessors. A study on the genetics of birds carried out in Sweden recorded that the mutation rates in males were between four and seven times higher than in females, which supports the view that evolution may well be driven by males.

That living things should exist at all, let alone make copies of themselves, is nothing short of wondrous.

Sex and immortality

Indeed, life is the only process in the world that builds, and the chemistry which maintains it is so precarious that organisms decay rapidly after death. From before the moment of birth a steady deterioration sets in – bodies inevitably become decrepit, joints and teeth wear out, arteries become clogged with fat, hearing fades and vision becomes blurred. These are the outward manifestations of wear and tear, but a more sinister form of corruption takes place as errors begin to accumulate in the body's chemistry. The chemistry begins as a finely tuned system but, with time, mistakes occur, especially when the DNA instructions are copied, as they must be in growing tissues. Although many of these errors are detected and repaired by the cells' own mechanisms, some blemished genes establish themselves until the accumulated flaws make the genetic instructions unreadable. Flawed DNA is responsible for cancers, leukaemia and inherited diseases such as haemophilia.

OVERLEAF Three generations in one: spherical *Volvox* colonies about to release daughter colonies, which already contain the next generation. Being clones, they are genetically similar.

If adult and ageing individuals faithfully passed on copies of their DNA to their offspring, after a few generations the accumulated errors would make life untenable. Sex – expensive and extravagant though it be – conquers death by filtering out undesirable and damaged genes. In sexual creatures, vastly more cells set out on the gamete production line than ever become fertilized. In females, those destined to form eggs are separated out very early in life before they have had a chance to be blighted with age-induced flaws. For instance, a woman sets aside about 100,000 potential egg cells while she is still inside her mother's womb, and these enter into a long metabolic sleep until a few hundred are eventually activated throughout her reproductive life. Males continuously produce billions of gametes. In the prolific sperm-making process, many will be faulty, especially in ageing males; the overwhelming majority will die on the way or fail to reach their target, leaving the field to a few vigorous and healthy ones. The sperm and egg which combine their genes are the survivors of a lengthy purging process which weeds out cells bearing deleterious mutations. And the cull does not stop there – many fertilized eggs fail to survive before they have a chance of producing imperfect bodies. As the embryo begins to materialize, fresh new cells as yet unspoilt by accidents in copying are reserved for gamete production, while the rest are destined for frequent multiplication and differentiation to make a mortal body.

The assorted shuffling of the genes in the egg- and sperm-production lines is a further system of quality control. Instead of being simply a duplicate of the cell that went before, a gamete results from a complicated event whereby the chromosomes of paternal and maternal origin line up and exchange lengths of DNA with each other. Each then receives a single set of chromosomes carrying a mixture of maternal and paternal genes.

Far from being primarily a means of reproduction, sex, according to one theory, may have been initially a way of 'proof-reading' DNA and mending errors. The process may have started as a co-operative venture between asexual microbes which possessed only a single copy of their genetic instructions. Any accumulation of errors would have confused their cellular chemistry and, without reference to the correct DNA sequences, would have made any kind of repair difficult. Such creatures needed to match their own instructions against those of an undamaged set. Getting together with a neighbour and checking each other's genes might have solved the problem by showing up differences. This might ultimately have led to every cell possessing two sets of chromosomes – one from either parent – with every gene 'backed up' with another copy. Should one be faulty, then the alternative gene was likely to be perfectly serviceable.

But although this mechanism might show how sex purges harmful mutations, it does not fully explain why the process persists.

Male, female or just plain mating types

When teasing apart the details of sexual behaviour, it is crucial to identify the participants. To us, the obvious candidates practising sex belong to either of the two genders – male or female. But the simple association of sex and the two genders is misleading. If the concept of maleness and femaleness is banished in favour of 'mating types', then the natural world can be explored to see whether there exist any organisms which have more than two. Such is the diversity of nature that animals which seem to have several 'sexes' do occur. Although they are not widespread, various kinds of microbes have populations divided into more than two 'mating types'. The unicellular alga *Chlamydomonas*, myriads of which often colour stagnant water with the green colour of their chloroplasts, as well as the predatory slipper animalcule *Paramecium*, occur in many strains. Each functions like an individual gender because individuals can exchange genetic material – or 'mate' – only with strains other than their own. Slime moulds – organisms like amoeba which live on rotten wood and which coalesce into mushroom-like reproductive bodies –

display no fewer than thirteen mating types. In the isopod crustacean *Paracerceis sculpta*, a marine relative of the familiar wood lice, there are three male 'sexes', each using a different strategy to mate. Alpha males are big and strong with tough spiny tails; each defends a cavity in a sponge where he sequesters three or four females. Beta males resemble weakly armoured females and fool the large guardian males into accepting them as potential mates. Once inside the harems, they surreptitiously mate with the females. Gamma males are the third sort of male; although dwarfs, they are recognized as competitors by the alpha males, which try and exclude them from their chambers. However, these little rakes are extremely fast swimmers and frequently get past the defending males; they then lurk inside the sponge, where they fertilize the females.

A curious situation also prevails in a much more advanced creature – a rodent. Wood lemmings of the high northern coniferous forests and tundra seem to be differentiated into four mating types; some are orthodox males, but the 'females' appear to belong to one of three 'sexes', one of which produces only daughters, presumably to enable the population to increase rapidly when conditions are favourable.

Fascinating though these examples are, the great majority of animals, like those that went into Noah's Ark, have only two mating types, to which we assign identifiable characteristics and call them male and female – the sexes. So why do most organisms live and breed in two gender-specific sexes, and how did the situation evolve? The answer illuminates the very nature of the battle which is the subject of this book and possibly the greatest of all motivational forces – competition.

Protosex and the origin of gender

Although the origins of the two genders are obscured by the mists of time, the sexual process is probably at least a billion years old – perhaps going back to a period when only single-celled creatures stirred themselves in the antediluvian seas. Present-day microbes undoubtedly differ from their distant ancestors, but they might provide some clues as to how non-sexual microbes became differentiated into males and females.

For most of the time, protozoa such as *Paramecium* multiply by binary fission – they simply split into 'daughter' cells which are identical to the parent. However, occasionally – and especially when their environment starts to deteriorate – these microscopic organisms seek partners and temporarily join up with them in a process called conjugation. The individuals then swap some of their cell contents with each other, so that when they part they are constitutionally changed. Afterwards each

Paramecium may metamorphose into a resilient and long-lasting spore. Conjugation is a primitive form of sex in which there is no outward sign of the division into separate genders. But it is possible to speculate how, from this situation, males and females might have arisen through 'cheating'.

Single-celled gametes function in extremely competitive environments; their success is measured by how quickly they can intercept a compatible partner with which to fuse their genes. In the beginning, when all gametes looked identical – perhaps like *Paramecium* – those which skimped on their internal stores were able to swim a little faster than the rest and might have found a partner more quickly. In time, these 'cheats' which 'selfishly' avoided making an equal contribution to the next generation evolved into slimmed-down sperms – each reduced to a powerful motor to propel a package of genes as fast as possible to its target. Apart from its DNA, a sperm, then as now, has no other resources to hand on.

With the evolution of a class of skinny but fast-moving cheats, other cell types were driven to compensate by becoming bloated with sufficient food to fulfil the entire task of nourishing the new life formed by the union. This class of gamete evolved into the relatively massive and immobile egg. Thus two genders were inevitably born out of the inherent rivalry that exists between living things, and from this basic differentiation between primitive mating types stem the strife, the deception and the manoeuvring for advantage that characterize the relationship between the sexes. Mirroring their own gametes, females tend to sink their resources into a limited number of yolky eggs. As eggs are biologically dearer to make, and in limited supply, females – as we have seen – became very discriminating over the quality of their male partners. For the first time, individuals were driven to making choices. By contrast, males manufacture myriads of sperm which, being minuscule and lacking provisions, are cheap to produce and individually less valuable – and so males have nothing to lose by scattering them around. Indeed, they can make huge reproductive gains by fertilizing as many females as possible. The tension arising out of the differing strategies between males and females, which stems from the very nature of their gametes, is what energizes the battle between the sexes.

Worlds apart! And yet these tiny planktonic crustaceans represent one of the ultimate expressions of sexual dimorphism. The female *Copilia* (left) resembles a typical copepod – she is a free swimming predator – but the male (right) is thought to be a parasite living inside salps.

But what was originally so advantageous about sex that it caused primitive life forms to forsake simple splitting for the complexities of separate genders? Today, we and the majority of our fellow creatures have no option but to procreate by sex and to put up with the consequences. Years ago, eminent zoologists such as John Maynard-Smith of Sussex University questioned the then orthodox explanation for sex – namely that it was a generator of variable offspring which would 'benefit the species'. It had to be good for passing on the individual's genes. He pointed out that, for the majority of females, producing broods which were more or less 50 per cent male was largely a waste because most would never breed – only one in 10 red deer stags ever manages to father any offspring, for example. Furthermore, male activity is often counter-productive to effective motherhood; belligerent males occasionally batter babies or kill them – deliberately or accidentally. Nevertheless, sex is so universally established that the system must have redeeming qualities which transcend the drawbacks and encourage animals to stick with it.

One clue to its use is the vulnerability of clones to diseases caused by sexually reproducing parasites. A good example from the plant world was the speed with which potatoes were virtually wiped out in Ireland by a killer blight; the result was the Great Famine of 1845–6, when over a million people starved to death. The Irish crop, like the modern King Edward potato, was more or less a clone and had no resistance to the infection. Sexual spuds might not have succumbed so easily, according to William D. Hamilton of the University of Oxford, who has proposed the latest and most intriguing explanation for sex – that it evolved as a strategic weapon in the arms race between rapidly breeding and short-lived parasites and their hosts. In other words, sex helps us all to combat the ever-present threat of disease.

Sex and the ultimate arms race

Sex is most prevalent in species which live in the complex and very variable tropics where microbes and parasites abound. It is more likely to be relinquished where life is fairly simple and predictable, such as on the tundra, in the depths of the sea or up mountains.

For the majority of living things, the world is not a congenial place. Since time immemorial, every animal and plant has been beleaguered by a host of microbes – viruses, fungi, bacteria and tiny parasites – reflecting the truth of Jonathan Swift's famous ditty '... a Flea hath smaller Fleas that on him prey; and these have smaller fleas to bite 'em and so proceed *ad infinitum*'. Whereas most of these micro-organisms are innocuous, many are potentially dangerous. Indeed, at the end of the day, a songbird is in much less peril from a falcon swooping out of the sky, or a zebra from a lion leaping from cover, than either is from the myriads of unseen but lethal pathogens and parasites battling to settle on their bodies or to invade and set up home in their tissues. The latter types specialize in burglary – picking biochemical 'locks', breaking into cells, consuming their contents or, like viruses, taking over the genetic machinery and reprogramming it to manufacture more viruses. Each kind of parasite is covered by a coat of special proteins which sometimes prevents the host from recognizing it as an alien, allowing it to multiply with impunity. These surface proteins also behave like keys which bind on to the host's cell walls, and help the microbes to slip inside and exploit the rich contents. But the hosts fight back, attempting to foil the foreign invaders by altering the details of their biochemical locks. As a consequence, over generations, the pathogens relentlessly change their 'coats' so that they can once again unlock their host's defences. In this, the ultimate arms race in nature, a biological détente prevails in which neither host nor pathogen wins, but neither can the contestants afford to relax.

In theory, the battalions of bacteria and viruses ought to win the race hands down because, although the individuals are microscopic, they have such a rapid turnover of generations that they can mutate faster than their hosts, which are engaged in a much slower reproductive schedule. For this reason, influenza viruses, for example, are able to outsmart – by a huge margin – the ability of their long-lived hosts to counter-attack, thereby causing a great deal of human misery. But, on the whole, something keeps the hosts level pegging in their ability to retaliate – and that something is sex.

In 1973, Leigh Van Allen, an ecologist at the University of Chicago, likened this stalemate to the Red Queen's race with Alice in Lewis Carroll's children's fantasy *Through the Looking Glass*. This formidable monarch runs like the wind but gets nowhere. Alice finds herself panting alongside the Queen in a topsy-turvy world where nothing is what it seems. 'Now, here, you see,' says the Red Queen to Alice, 'it takes all the running you can do to keep in the same place.' The notion that sexual reproduction might be responsible for the deadlock in the endless race of adaptive one-upmanship has become enshrined as the 'Red Queen Hypothesis'. Sex enables individuals to stay in the same place – that is, to survive.

The full advantage of sex is seen at the biochemical level. Individuals who are able to scramble and recombine their genes with a mate can maintain a perpetual genetic flux. They hand on to their offspring a bewildering variety of different biochemical locks, which prevent injurious germs from doing their worst. Sex therefore gives the hosts a decent chance of outwitting fast-breeding microbes and parasites – at least in the short term. Inevitably the infectious organisms will conjure up fresh surface proteins – new keys for opening the cellular locks – but, given the tremendous variation between individual hosts, they will not necessarily be effective in every one of them.

Long-lived creatures such as mammals possess immunological defences as well. The lymphocytes (white blood cells), for example, which play a key role in the defence of our bodies, are able to change rapidly to recognize and attack invasions of fresh pathogens. In fact, the immune system constantly refashions the cellular and biochemical environment that virulent microbes and parasites face inside their hosts. But like almost everything else, the properties of the immune system are laid down by the genes, and so are subject to innovation from one generation to another through the creative process of sexual reproduction.

Sickle cell – sex's cure for malaria

Evidence for the arms race between hosts and parasites comes from research into scourges such as malaria. The disease is produced when mosquitoes inject one or other form of the *Plasmodium* microbes into the bloodstream, where they later infect and destroy red corpuscles. When the corpuscles periodically burst and release the parasites *en masse* into the blood, the victim suffers the debilitating fevers characteristic of the disease. Worldwide, more than 100 million people a year contract malaria; about one and a half million of them die. With humans and *Plasmodium* parasites competing on such a scale, the evolution of each is bound to have been shaped by the other.

Being born with the sickle-cell anaemia gene is a consequence of sexual reproduction. Those who inherit a copy of this gene from both their mother and their father die young, because their red blood cells are packed with a faulty form of haemoglobin which has a low affinity for oxygen. However, carriers of just a single copy have a relatively high proportion of normal haemoglobin and so survive. Although uncommon in most races, the gene is prevalent in black Africans and those descended from them. In Gambia, for instance, about one in four of the population carries the sickle-cell anaemia gene.

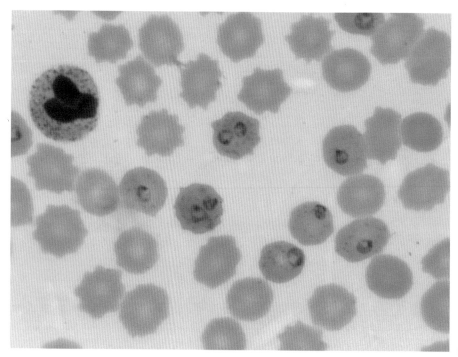

LEFT Mass murderer. Injected into the blood by mosquitoes, the malaria parasite has killed more people than all other diseases and warfare combined. Sex might help us fight microbes like this.

RIGHT A ruddy complexion in uakari monkeys signals good health and resistance to monkey malaria. Pale-faced ones are sickly and have no sex appeal.

The distribution of the gene was something of a mystery until it was discovered that those carrying a single copy were pretty well immune to malaria, because enough of their red blood corpuscles were too distorted to allow rampant infection. As the benefits of being resistant to malaria more than outweighed the mortality from sickle-cell anaemia, natural selection favoured the gene in African populations afflicted by the disease, instead of eliminating it. Quite simply, having a single copy of the gene in malaria-infested swamps and forests is a great advantage. It has been estimated that it may prevent the equivalent of 12 per cent of all serious cases in certain regions of Africa.

The malaria parasite also varies in its effectiveness. Over nine out of ten deaths from malaria are caused by *Plasmodium falciparum* – an exceptionally virulent strain of blood parasite. Biochemically, this differs from the less lethal forms and may be more closely related to the organisms that affect birds. Indeed, *Plasmodium falciparum* may have been acquired from avian carriers some time during the past 10,000 years and the human population has not yet evolved an effective immunological defence against it. A great deal more sex is required!

Red faces in the jungle

In the Brazilian rain-forest, those who have studied uakari monkeys have discovered clues that link the needs for sexual reproduction and the battle against malaria. Uakari monkeys are the least known of all primates, because most of them live in the remote reaches of the Amazon, where a thousand and one tributaries rise and fall with the seasons, annually flooding great swathes of forest. By most human standards of beauty, uakari rank among the most hideous forms of life on Earth. Each has a stumpy tail and spidery body hidden beneath a cloak of coarse, shaggy hair. However, the 'naked' head is what makes these arboreal creatures unique among monkeys. With so little subcutaneous fat to pad out the cheeks, the skin seems to be stretched over the underlying bone to hug the contours of the skull. There are two distinct races of the bald uakari, distinguished by the colour of their coats. One sports gingery brown fur and the other silvery grey or white. But their most interesting feature is the colour of their bare, bony faces, which look par-boiled.

Although uakari behaviour is poorly understood, its glowing face seems to be its beacon of beauty – the redder the face, the higher the animal's sex appeal. The males have the brightest faces and those whose heads are well flushed with blood are most successful in acquiring mates. By contrast, male uakaris with pallid complexions are forced to lead relatively celibate lives. Recent research has revealed that the colour is a reliable indicator of health and therefore fitness to breed. Living in the canopy of the flooded forest, the bald uakaris are continually bitten by mosquitoes, some of which transmit the blood parasites which cause a strain of malaria unique to monkeys in this part of the world. The affliction shows up in the face; those uakaris which have contracted the disease look jaundiced – a poor prospect for any monkey looking for a mate. Accordingly, such pallid individuals are passed over in favour of robust-looking uakaris with healthy red complexions. We do not know whether these highly coloured animals possess a gene – like the sickle-cell anaemia gene – which protects them from the ravages of the parasite.

But there is a clever twist to the story. Not all uakaris clamber around the flooded forest. Some live in drier regions where mosquitoes and monkey malaria are much less prevalent. Remarkably, all these uakaris have black faces. As they live in an environment where they are absolved from battling against a crippling ailment, they have no need for a system of sexual signals which demonstrates that they are free from it – none of them contracts malaria. Presumably, they have evolved something else to advertise their fitness, of which nothing is known: the black-faced uakari is literally the most mysterious monkey on Earth.

Wriggling out of sex

Much of life on Earth is coupled to a form of reproduction involving the participation of two sexes because it has immense survival value. At each mating, genes are shuffled like cards in a pack to create another clutch of individually different offspring. But what if the genes of the parents are perfectly serviceable, and if the conditions in their surroundings never vary significantly? Under these circumstances, sex might suddenly become a liability, not only breaking up perfectly good combinations of genes, but also involving the participants in utterly wasteful practices. If sex becomes a bad thing, can animals wriggle out of it? For some, the answer, remarkably, is 'yes'.

Most higher animals which plump for celibacy appear to have relinquished sex quite recently, because they often retain traces of their sexual ancestry. Amazon mollies are a case in point. These are colourful little fish which live in streams in Mexico and Texas. As their name suggests, all members of this species are female. When mature, they produce only daughters, which are exact genetic copies of their mothers. And yet Amazon mollies fail to live up to the reputation of their human namesake of a completely self-reliant race of super-females. Although male Amazons are unknown, the female mollies indulge in a secret sex life with males of the related but sexual sailfin mollies. The reason seems to be that the eggs of the Amazon molly must be penetrated by sperm and scavenge a small length of chromosome from it to kick-start their embryonic development; apparently the sperm's genes are not incorporated into the resulting offspring. This curious state of affairs is clearly an evolutionary hangover from the recent past when these fish were conventionally sexual. Although males have been dispensed with, the future of this top minnow hinges upon the female's success in seducing males of related species and fooling them into releasing sperm – a practice of no benefit to the donors.

Such hangovers occur in many parthenogens (creatures which reproduce without the need for fertilization). Among plants, many reproduce without the involvement of sex, including that cosmopolitan and extremely common 'weed', the dandelion. From their abundance, these plants appear to be blessed with a robust set of genes and, in the interests of preserving them,

Who needs males? All whip-tailed lizards are females and reproduce asexually. But they still have fun, taking it in turns to mount each other like males to stimulate egg production.

have gone celibate. Although dandelions no longer need to be pollinated, they still invest resources into producing brilliant yellow flowers and sugary nectar to attract and 'pay' insects for a service that is no longer needed. The presence of flowers is probably an indication that dandelions have only recently given up sex – perhaps during the last few million years at the most.

Perhaps the most 'advanced' animal to dispense with sex for breeding purposes is the whip-tailed lizard, which lives in the deserts of the south-western United States. Here, the conditions are harsh but predictable and apparently the pressure from pathogens is relatively low, so the benefits of genetic shuffling do not seem to be essential for the survival of a healthy population of whip-tails. The females clone themselves and produce identical daughters. Without the need to make sons, these virginal reptiles are able to double their reproductive potential.

'Lesbian' lizards

However, as in the case of Amazon mollies, whip-tails carry a physiological legacy from the time when they were fully sexual, and this presents them with a complication. The females must engage in 'lesbian' couplings in order to stimulate egg production. Females which are not yet ready to breed take on the role of 'pseudomales' and go into the full courtship routine of a male lizard. At the sight of a female in breeding fettle, the pseudomale scampers after her, seizes her by the scruff of her neck and coils 'his' body round hers in an act of simulated copulation. This lasts for several minutes and apparently stimulates the secretion of hormones necessary for speeding the release of eggs. The only puzzle posed by these much studied and fascinating reptiles is why females should go through the motion of mating when they are not ready to clone themselves. Perhaps some kind of reciprocity is involved; the females are able to switch roles and so do each other sexual favours. A fully sexual female is thus able to mount and excite her former pseudomale lover when 'he' is ready to produce eggs. The other explanation is that many populations of these whip-tails are giant clones in which every individual is an exact genetic copy of the others, so there is no disadvantage to one lizard helping another to breed.

And yet parthenogens have clearly not inherited the earth. It has been estimated that, of the 3 million or so kinds of creatures which have been properly described, only about 1000 rely upon virgin birth to procreate. All this suggests that asexuality is favoured in species which are little troubled by disease, or where colonization and rapid population growth is at a premium.

True sex without dedicated males

It goes without saying that females have the monopoly on breeding. Only they have the ability to make new life by themselves; no male has been able to evolve a gamete which can grow into an adult organism in the way that a fully provisioned egg can. As, in an ideal world, females would pass on more of their genes by cloning yet more daughters like aphids, perhaps they have had to tolerate males as breeding partners in order to acquire the benefits of the sexual process. However, supposing females could reproduce *sexually* without involving a special caste of males? Hermaphrodite worms, slugs and snails do just that, but they have possibly never gone down the path of complex sex with separately differentiated males and females and all that goes with them. Like many animals without backbones, their bodies may always have contained both sets of gonads, and their spawning or coupling behaviour usually ensures cross-fertilization. A few vertebrates have managed to evolve such a bizarre arrangement, which is itself very remarkable indeed, because the ancestors of these creatures must have had separate males and females. The females of certain kinds of fish have taken this amazing reproductive initiative but, unlike virginal whip-tailed lizards and Amazon mollies, have retained the advantages of sex.

Perhaps the most unusual method is shown by one of the killifishes or toothed carps called *Rivulus mamroratus*. Found in the New World, ranging from Florida to Brazil, this species lays claim to being the only vertebrate with the ability to fertilize itself. Each fish has an ovotestis, with egg and sperm production taking place in adjacent tubules – although how the hormonal processes manage not to interfere with each other is baffling. Sperms are released into the interior lumen of the gonad and, when the comparatively large eggs are liberated during the normal process of ovulation, they are fertilized *in situ*. The process is so efficient that few, if any, unfertilized ones escape into the water at spawning time. By then, the fertilized eggs already contain developing embryos. Each produces a simultaneous hermaphrodite. Occasionally, at low temperatures, diminutive males are made, but they play no part in fathering the fry.

Quite clearly, these amazing little fish have uncoupled themselves from dedicated males while retaining the advantages of sex. By fertilizing themselves, they are retaining their own genes, although, by shuffling them in the sexual process, they produce offspring which are not clonal copies of the parents but variations on the same successful set of genes. Such limited variability is all that is possible without cross-fertilization with a caste of genetically different males. However, there are species which go one stage better and have the full benefits of sex without males.

Harlequin bass, *Serranus tigrinus*, live on reefs that fringe the Caribbean. They are related to the colourful little basslets (referred to in Chapter 1) which change sex from female to male according to their age and rank. However, harlequin bass are simultaneous hermaphrodites – each one is a properly kitted-out female but carries small testes as well. With two sets of gonads, each fish could presumably fertilize its own eggs, but harlequin bass 'choose' not to do so, opting instead for coupling with a carefully selected partner. As a way of breeding, simultaneous hermaphroditism with partners trading eggs or sperm seems ideal – at least the females do not waste 50 per cent of their effort making sons. Furthermore, by exchanging minimal amounts of semen and cross-fertilizing each other's eggs, the fish still profit from the advantages of sex by generating individually unique offspring, all of which can lay eggs.

OVERLEAF Time for a change. Some female grey seals may be in the process of modifying the harem arrangement, snubbing the warrior bulls which rule them in favour of gentler males and a system of non-violent monogamy.

Consorting in pairs and defending a territory, the harlequin bass take it in turns to spawn and shed milt as the situation requires. Like so many marine creatures, breeding peaks near the time of the full moon when, at sunset, each member of the pair behaves alternately as a male and as a female. The sequence is initiated by one fish – playing the female role – displaying 'her' body in the shape of an 'S' with her bulbous belly exposed to her partner, which might be several metres (yards) away. If sufficiently stimulated by the seductive posture, the partner swims towards the displaying fish and they both swim to the surface, one releasing eggs and the other a little puff of semen at the climax of the spawning rush. Then the roles are reversed – the female which has just released her eggs returns the favour by fertilizing the eggs voided by the former 'male'.

This ability of females to switch back and forth between both sexual roles is also found in a group of related Caribbean fishes – the hamlets. Some of these are mimics which have evolved into ten stable colour forms – or morphs – to resemble the black, blue or yellow damselfishes with which they keep company. Once considered to be separate species, they are now all lumped together as varieties of *Hypoplectrus unicolor*. Reproducing without proper males, they trade eggs with members of their own colour – for instance, black hamlets found in the reefs around Jamaica form pairs around dusk to spawn, the 'male' wrapping himself sensuously around the 'female' as the pair rise about a metre (yard) above the seabed where the gametes are released. The partners then switch sexual roles.

The mystery is why this method of reproduction is so rare. Perhaps among higher animals, fish are anatomically simple enough to retain two sets of functional gonads, whereas more advanced creatures are so structurally committed to one or other sexual role that the arrangement is not a practical proposition. Maybe it all comes down to this – if sex is an insurance against extinction, then dedicated males are the premium that females of most species have to pay for keeping their fecund daughters in the running!

The battle continues

By nature, the negotiation between the sexes is a dynamic process. The tension between males and females continues and, accordingly, the compromises struck between them in their quest for genetic supremacy are ever changing. The seeds of change can be detected on the rocky beaches of Rona on which grey seals breed. Rona is a small island well to the west of the Orkney Isles off the north coast of Scotland. At the best of times it is a wild and windy place, bearing the brunt of the Atlantic swell. In October, when the seals give birth and then immediately mate again, it is frequently lashed by gales; the exposed cliffs and gullies shudder under the pounding waves. But the appalling conditions are apparently of no consequence: Rona hosts the densest population of grey seals in the North Atlantic – about 600 breeding females.

The grey seal is a classical polygynous species with a very marked size difference between the sexes. Whereas every cow can expect to breed, the bulls are not so fortunate. Each one lives in the hope that one day he will be big enough and a sufficiently good fighter to win his own harem of cows. Sexual selection among bull grey seals has therefore favoured the most powerful pugilists, and the biggest warriors get their chance to mate with perhaps a dozen females each season. However, a few of the lesser bulls, which stand no chance of succeeding in combat, turn lucky – and it is all down to the cows. Although most happily fall for the victorious bulls, a minority of females take a fancy to the males of a more gentle disposition which lounge on the sidelines. Luckily grey seals can be recognized by their individual markings. It has therefore been possible to discover that these cows tend to return in successive years to the same males, and they appear to strike up monogamous 'marriages'.

Clearly two separate mating strategies are underway, but perhaps the female grey seals are beginning to exercise a preference for less disruptive and less heavy bulls to father their pups. If so, their choice is nudging evolution towards establishing monogamy in place of the current strongly polygamous arrangement. We know that the nature of habitats favours some breeding systems over others. Perhaps this is the case with these seals, which probably bred on sea ice during the last Ice Age. Now that the climate has improved and the ice retreated, grey seals may still be in the process of adapting to the change – and this includes establishing a new relationship between the sexes.

In conclusion, we can all be thankful for the sexual process. It is the most creative force on our planet. It not only maintains the chemistry of life, but also conjures up individual variations which are the fodder of natural selection – the engine of evolution. For perhaps 2000 billion years or more after the first signs of primitive organisms were seen, life on Earth changed very little. But, with the advent of sexual reproduction, evolution went into overdrive. Within a few hundred million years, all the major kinds of animals and plants appeared, conquering land, sea and air with an incredible diversity of bodily designs. The consequences which stemmed from the conflicting agendas of males and females have been nothing short of stupendous. Without the battle of the sexes, the dazzling colour, beauty and drama of life on our watery planet would be missing.

OVERLEAF Designed to dazzle. The male *Sapphirina* – similar to the copepod on page 202 – has an extraordinary body with many facets which split sunlight. Here photographed by a special technique, in the plankton he sparkles like a tiny diamond to attract females.

Sex also touches every aspect of our own lives. The passion, frustration and anger generated between men and women have been the inspiration for great works of art, whether it be sublime music, soulful poetry or profound literature. And the cut of our clothes, the way we organize our family lives and many of our social activities reflect the fact that we are a highly sexed species.

There is an intriguing cosmic prediction to be drawn from our earthly battle of the sexes. Without a doubt, somewhere in the unimaginable void of the universe, life thrives on some benign planet energized by the warmth of a gentle neighbouring star. Whatever those distant creatures might look like, they will certainly have evolved a method of replicating. The chances are that it will involve the participation of two mating types – and that they will be at loggerheads!

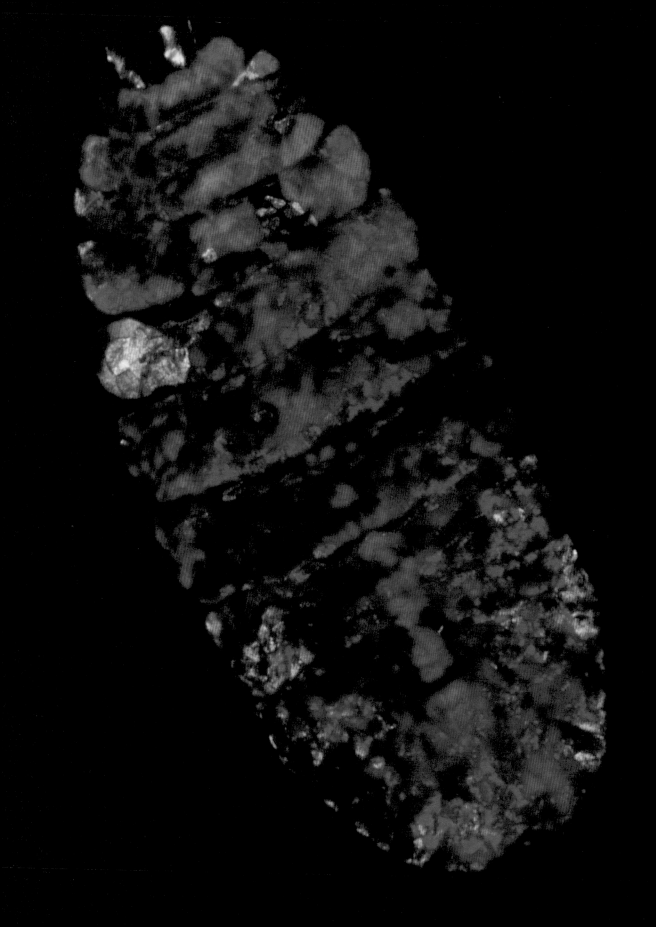

A large number of works of reference and scientific journals have been consulted in the writing of *Battle of the Sexes*. However, for those who may wish to pursue the topics covered in this book in more detail, the following list may be helpful.

BIRKHEAD, T.R., & A.P. MOLLER, *Sperm Competition in Birds*, Academic Press, 1992

> *Birds have proved to be ideal for studying many aspects of reproduction, including sperm competition – a central part of sexual selection. This is very much an authoritative treatment of the subject.*

DARWIN, CHARLES, *On The Origin of Species By Means Of Natural Selection*, John Murray, 1859
The Descent of Man and Selection in Relation to Sex, John Murray, 1871

> *Everyone should at least dip into Darwin. The intellectual framework for* Battle of the Sexes *was firmly explained by this extra-ordinary Victorian naturalist who, overnight, established our proper relationship with the rest of life on Earth. He is still a wonderful read. Try the first edition of the* On The Origin of Species *which is much more concise than subsequent ones. There are a number of reprints, including facsimile editions.*

DAVIS, N.B., *Dunnock Behaviour and Social Evolution*, Oxford University Press,1992

> *An amazing study of this little brown garden bird which reveals how the selfish interests of individuasl are translated into a whole range of sexual relationships. The very essence of* Battle of the Sexes.

DAWKINS, RICHARD, *The Selfish Gene*, Oxford University Press, 1989

> *An excellent read.The author explains in easy language how genes manage to preserve themselves at the expense of the bodies that carry them.*

The Blind Watchmaker, Penguin, 1990

> *This spells out how very complex living things and behaviours, which appear to be 'designed', are the products of the aimless process of natural selection.*

GOULD, JAMES L. & C.G., *Sexual Selection*, Scientific American Library, 1989

> *An excellent and well-illustrated survey of the subject.*

JOHNSGARD, PAUL, *Arena Birds. Sexual Selection and Behaviour*, Smithsonian Institution Press, 1994

> *A scientific monograph of the fascinating species which 'lek'– such as grouse, pheasants, some ducks and waders, manakins and birds of paradise.*

JONES, STEVE, *The Language of the Genes*, Harper Collins,1993

> *An entertaining account by a professor of genetics about genes, evolution and human history – a book to curl up with.*

KREBS, J.R., & DAVIES, N.B., *An Introduction to Behavioural Ecology*, Blackwell, 1993 (3rd edn.)

> *For those who wish to dig into the ecological backdrop of behaviour. Although a textbook for university students, this is an eminently accessible account.*

LUNDBERG, ARNE, & R.V. ALATALO, *The Pied Flycatcher*, T. & A.D. Poyser, 1992

> *The detailed story of a species in which males, pursuing their reproductive potential, set up mistresses but then desert them in favour of their wives!*

RIDLEY, MATT, *The Red Queen. Sex and the Evolution of Human Nature*, Viking, London, 1993

> *This book traces with great clarity the recent*

transformation of evolutionary biology by the 'Red Queen Hypothesis': evolution is not about 'progress', but sex – a vital weapon in disease resistance – enables species to change in order 'to stay in the same place'.

SHORT, R.V., & E. BALABAN (EDITORS) *'The Differences Between the Sexes.'* Cambridge University Press, 1994

A series of articles by leading experts presenting

an overview of the subject. They range across sex change in fish, the evolution of male weapons, the behaviour of elephants and the costs of sex in red deer. Chiefly for undergraduates.

WILSON, EDWARD O, *The Insect Societies*, Harvard University Press, 1971

A marvellous treatise on social insects, well illustrated and in the distinguished author's easily assimilable style.

PICTURE CREDITS

BBC Books would like to thank the following for providing photographs and for permission to reproduce copyright material. While every effort has been made to trace and acknowledge all copyright holders, we would like to apologize should there have been any errors or omissions.

ARDEA pp. 86 *top* (John Daniels), 126 (Pascal Goetgheluck), 130 (Joanna van Gruisen) & 138 (Ferrero-Labat); AUSCAPE pp. 87 *right* (Jean-Paul Ferrero) & 179 (Roger Brown); BBC NATURAL HISTORY UNIT pp. 30 (Jeff Rotman), 46 (Richard Kirby), 79 (Duncan McEwan), 83 (Anup Shah), 109-10 (Jeff Foott), 127 (Premaphotos), 154 *bottom* (Andrew Murray) & 183 (Andrew Murray); BIOPHOTO ASSOCIATES p. 206; BRUCE C0LEMAN COLLECTION pp. 6 (Johnny Johnson), 15 *left* (Jane Burton), 55 (Marie Read), 67 (Alain Compost), 90 (Eckart Pott), 106 (Waina Cheng Ward), 158-9 (Rod Williams), 162-3 (Erwin & Peggy Bauer), 194 (Kim Taylor), 207 (Rod Williams) & 214-15 (Rob Jordan); RICHARD DU TOIT p. 178; FLPA pp. 134 *left* (A.R.Hamblin) & 135 (John Hawkins); MICHAEL & PATRICIA FOGDEN pp. 15 *right*, 75 top, 103 & 122 *inset*; JOHN B.FREE p. 167; DAVID H. FUNK p. 50 *main picture*; ROBERT HARDING PICIURE LIBRARY p. 42; IMAGE QUEST 3-D/PETER PARKS pp. 78, 115 *both*, 186-7, 190, 191 *both*, 198-9, 202 & 218; MINDEN PICTRES pp. 10-11 (Mark Moffett) & 19 (Mark Moffett); NHPA pp. 43 (A.P.Barnes), 146-7

(Nigel J.Dennis), 150 (E.A.Janes) & 171 (Martin Harvey); OXFORD SCIENTIFIC FILMS pp. 2-3 (Matthias Breiter), 26 (Mark Deeble & Victoria Stone), 47 (Peter Cathercole), 51 (Norbert Rosing), 58 (Liz & Tony Bomford),70-1 (Martyn Colbeck), 87 *left* (Babs & Bert Wells), 91 (Mantis Wildlife Films/Densey Cline), 114 (Ben Osborne), 118 (Mark Deeble & Victoria Stone), 119 (Rudie Kuiter), 134 *right* (Ennio Boga), 142-3 *main picture* (Andrew Plumptre), 154 *top* (Clive Bromhall), 166 (Raymond A.Mendez), 174 (Survival Anglia/Joe Blossom), 182 (Martyn Colbeck) & 210 (Phil Devries); PLANET EARTH PICTURES pp. 23 (Peter Scoones), 31 (Carl Roessler), 35 (Peter David), 66 (Beth Davidow), 95 (Norbert Wu), 98-9 (Herwarth Voigtmann), 139 (Jonathan Scott), 143 *inset* (Jonathan Scott) & 151 (Jonathan Scott); PREMAPHOTOS pp. 34, 50 *inset*, 74 & 75 *bottom* (all Ken Preston-Mafham); JOHN RUTHVEN pp. 62-3 & 86 *bottom* ; PHIL SAVOIE pp. 22, 38-9, 102 *both* & 112 *main picture*; BARRY SINERVO p. 27 *all*; STILL PICTURES p. 155(Xavier Eichaker); STOCK MARKET p. 14.

The drawing on p. 84 is by Birgitte Bruun and comes from Jens Rasmussen, 'On two little-known African water snakes' (*Crotaphopeltis degeni* and *C. Barotseensis*) in *Amphibia-Reptilia*, Vol.18, 1997. © Koninklijke Brill, Leiden.

INDEX